Schwelien · Encounter and Encouragement

Early immigrant from Germany—today they look different

Joachim H. Schwelien

Encounter
and
Encouragement

A Bicentennial
Review
of German–American
Relations

The author, who is solely responsible for the contents of this booklet, wishes to express his gratitude to the offices and departments of the United States government and the government of the Federal Republic of Germany which assisted in collecting factual material related to the history of German-American relations over the centuries.

Differences and similarities

In the period since the end of World War II, Americans have viewed the Federal Republic of Germany as a re-emerging economic giant which, in the eyes of the world, nevertheless moves like a political dwarf. Germans, on the other hand, regard the United States —despite sporadic doubts about its role of leadership in international politics—as a superpower whose vitality and protection remain indispensable to Germany's security and existence.

The images that the two countries hold of each other are subject to continuous change—analogous to the changes that occur in their relations and in the constellation of political power among the major nations on this earth. But even under these conditions of change, relations between the German and the American peoples are relatively stable. Especially at the present time when the relaxation of tensions between East and West must stand the endurance test of practical politics in which entirely new geographical and economic dimensions of cooperation—but also of conflict—emerge, the United States and the Federal Republic of Germany feel a need to work together hand in hand as friends. The real bases for this cooperation are as convincing today as ten or twenty years ago. This recognition always prevails when Germans and Americans of considered opinion sit around a table and soberly and objectively weigh their thoughts on the relations between the two nations.

On such occasions, they almost always share the conviction that as relations between the United States and the Federal Republic are adjusted to the course of events corrections should be directed —without neglect of their cooperation in multinational alliances and agreements—towards an intensification of their bilateral cooperation.

It should not be overlooked that sometimes experts have been inclined to recommend a drastic intensification of German-American bilateral ties. For example, during a meeting of politicians, economists and political scientists, Fred Bergsten (a noted member of the Brookings Institution) suggested a German-American economic "bigemony", or a union of the two countries, which would be a little weaker than a condominium but considerably stronger than a partnership. Although his concept was criticized by most of the partipants as too far fetched, it indicated the broad range of options which are open in relations between the Federal Republic of Germany and the USA.

German-American relations have undergone an immense change since the end of World War II, when Secretary of the Treasury Henry Morgenthau proposed that Germany be transformed into an agricultural state. Instead, the United States pumped massive economic aid into Western Germany to help it rebuild its industry. The Federal Republic has meanwhile become a full member of the NATO defense alliance. And now, West German Chiefs of Government confer bilaterally with American presidents on problems of international security, measures for overcoming international economic crises and on steps for coping with energy supply problems. They have even searched together for ways to close the gap between the highly developed industrialized states and the nations of the Third World. In those years of transition, relations between the two countries underwent a continuous evolution. This process has by no means either been completed or suspended. On the contrary, it continues to move ahead.

This is why the event of the American Bicentennial of 1976 appears to be an appropriate opportunity for taking stock of what Germans and Americans have meant to each other in the course of the centuries and for contemplating what they can mean to each other in the future; what brings them together and what divides them, what they have in common and how they differ. Contemporary history develops the framework of future history. But the mere fact that one type of relationship exists between two countries at present does not at all make it possible to make cocksure predictions of how this relationship will be in the far distant future. Whether in the coming decades the Germans and Americans will move arm in arm, whether they will go their own or parallel ways or, perhaps, even once again develop in opposition to each other depends primarily on their individual spheres of interest. This is a fundamental factor in relations between individual states.

In addition to this, however, many other factors play a no less important role: affinities, for example, or differences in the characters of the two peoples, stereotyped notions about the other side, emotions and evaluations as well as spontaneous changes in the political philosophies of the younger generation, which rebels today and leads tomorrow. In our inspection of the Germans and Americans—which in such limited space can only touch on a few of the significant elements of the historical and present development of this relationship— we must pay equal attention to the constant as well as the variable factors. For, today one thing is absolutely certain: regardless of how they may develop, the state of relations between the Federal Republic of Germany and the United States is of vital importance to both nations.

One other factor is just as certain: in official dealings, West Germany is virtually an equal partner of the United States. Recognizing this, Washington often seeks the advice and support of its German ally. On the other hand, this German State is by no means in precisely the same category of nations as the United States. Completely aside from all well-known and obvious differences between the two (geographical size, population, economic and military potential, overall output, accomplishment, regional activities and global responsibilities), beyond them it is a fact that the security of the Federal Republic depends to a very special and large degree on the United States. This situation should be absolutely clear to all.

On the other hand, the dependency of the Germans in the Federal Republic on the attitude or conduct of America is not to be mistaken for helpless subordination. Quite to the contrary, it merely creates mutual dependency of the one on the other. Indeed, the economic capacity of the 62 million Germans in the Federal Republic and West Berlin, their military potential and the political influence of their government make West Germany an important member of the international community. But above all, West Germany's unique geographical situation as the more substantial part of a divided nation bordering on the powerful Soviet Union and its allies make the Federal Republic of Germany an important factor in Central Europe.

If West Germany were to change its status and, for example, become neutral or dependent on Eastern Europe, the balance of power in Europe would be decisively altered. At the moment there is no substitute for West Germany's reliance on the United States. The Federal Republic could not exist without America's protection, at least not as long as there is no unified Western Europe strong enough to stand completely on its own feet in which West Germany surely would be incorporated. And the chain-reaction of events which President John F. Kennedy forsaw should there be a lessening of this close interdependency still holds. He believed that if America were to be forced out of West Berlin, this would inevitably be followed by the loss of the Federal Republic and eventually also by the loss of all of Western Europe. The ensuing isolation of the United States, he believed, would constitute a perilous threat to the entire American continent.

During a visit to West Berlin in the summer of 1975, Secretary of State Henry Kissinger made clear that this theory still stands. In the divided city, he said, West Berlin is living proof that the United States keeps its word. The city, he continued, has meanwhile acquired another symbolic significance that détente can work. And, he concluded, "Only if Berlin flourishes will détente flourish; only if you are secure will Europe be secure."

To be sure, he could easily have extended this to apply not only to Europe but also to America. For, dependency on each other of two nations of such differing weight as West Germany and the United States is a long-term affair and the result of necessities which can be expanded or limited by sentiments or moods but which cannot, however, be eliminated altogether.

The interdependency which has emerged over the past three decades is not confined solely to economic interlacement, to joint defense policies or to the nuclear umbrella provided by the United States for West Germany's ultimate security. It goes much deeper and farther than that: all the way to the two countries' domestic politics and their concepts for bringing about social change. The influences and effects which student revolts in Germany and America have had on each other are just as unmistakable as the drastic changes of direction which the political parties have been compelled to make as the result of the emergence of a joint defense policy. As the governing party, the Social Democratic Party of Germany (SPD), for example, supports West Germany's membership in NATO and its contribution to the defense activities of the alliance with the same verve as the SPD's predecessor in government, the conservative Christian Democratic Union (CDU/CSU), did under Konrad Adenauer. This is the SPD's position today, regardless of the fact that at first (and in view of their traditional development) the Social Democrats quite understandably opposed German rearmament.

Young German critics of America's Indochina policy and German liberals armed themselves with some of the ideas and arguments of the anti-war and cívil rights movements in America bent on domestic reform. It is therefore incorrect to view their criticism of restless America as basically anti-American in nature, especially since many of the ideas they adopted in fact were born somewhere between Berkeley and New York.

Short and to the point: whether Germans and Americans love or hate each other, whether they study or ignore each other; all of that is less significant than what is the decisive characteristic of their present relations, namely that they simply cannot do without each other in the current phase of history. And it is quite inconsequential whether this applies more to the one side or more to the other.

The present situation was brought about in the twentieth century by two decisive chains of developments. Though it was indeed a great power, the United States was not yet a world power when it entered the first World War in 1917 and prevented the collapse of the Western Alliance and thereby assisted in reestablishing a balance of power in Europe. But this balance is considerably different from the one which had existed prior to World War I. Eventually this new balance began to waver because, among other things (with its refusal to enter the League of Nations favored by President Woodrow Wilson, or to fully engage itself in the establishment of a new balance of power in Europe) the United States had withdrawn into what amounted to a type of semi-isolationism which probably was one of the many elements leading to the annihilating second World War.

Hitler's advance to the coast of the English Channel and to the skies above London unavoidably raised the question for Washington as to how German control of the Atlantic coast would affect America's own security. We need not enter into the continuing controversy concerning the real origins and causes of the two World Wars or who bears responsibility for them. The opinions range from former Secretary of State Dean Acheson's version of two European civil wars to the belief in sole German responsibility. But there is no question that these two global armed conflicts had a completely undeniable and certainly unexpected side-effect: the emergence of the United States as a world power.

The two World Wars which originated in and around Germany brought the United States out of its isolationism and forced it into its role as a global power. By contributing decisively to the defeat of the Axis Powers, the U.S. aided the creation of a power vacuum in Europe. America, in turn, had to fill this vacuum itself in order to prevent the intrusion of an antagonistic power. That power eventually emerged as a second world superpower known today as the Soviet Union. So, the events which originated in Germany were equally responsible for the rise of America to a world power as well as the continuing rivalry between the United States and the Soviet Union and to present efforts to equalize interests through accomodation and détente.

A German estimation of the postion and rank the Federal Republic occupies as a partner of the United States could be of interest to Americans. This is probably most true of Americans who do not have much opportunity to consider for themselves the weight which West Germany carries in the political deliberations of the United States because their attention is focused primarily on events within the confines of their own country or elsewhere in the world. There are no explosive points of contention or disputes between Bonn and Washington. The Federal Republic enjoys a relatively high degree of domestic, political and economic stability and consequently usually does not make headlines in the American mass media. For these reasons, the topic of West Germany is hardly likely to engage or capture the attention of the American public. And this certainly is no cause for concern.

Nevertheless, in relations between states there are many other effective layers of influence which are not immediately evident. If one takes them all into consideration, then one cannot escape the conclusion that the Federal Republic of Germany, indeed, is among those nations which are of primary importance to America and, vice versa, that America is of principal importance to West Germany. Just a few but solid facts prove this: for example, for some time the United States has maintained larger numbers of troops on West German territory than in any other region in the world. West Germany has become one of America's largest transatlantic trade and capital investment partners. Tourism between the two countries continues to increase, as does the exchange of cultural and political visitors between the two capitals.

In addition to these purely bilateral ties, in many multilateral organizations Germans and Americans together are often the brace within the Western Community which produces an equalization of interests and from which joint initiatives emanate. This is the case in such forums as the Organization for Economic Cooperation and Development (OECD), the World Bank, the World Monetary Fund and the United Nations. It also happens in the less permanent conferences such as those in Helsinki and in Vienna on achieving Security and Cooperation in Europe (CSCE) and a Mutual and Balanced Forces Reduction (MBFR). Within the European Community (EC), which has its share of conflicts with the United States, West Germany is the member which is most ready to take into account the American position before coming to a conclusion.

West Germany has certain limitations in freedom of movement in orienting its own basic foreign policy, but it carries considerable weight in the formulation of the European Community's foreign policy. Sometimes—in the interests of the goal of achieving political unity in Western Europe—Bonn goes along with Community decisions which are not necessarily to Washington's liking. This was the case, for example, with the European Community's adoption of a balanced, neutral position on the Middle East conflict which reflected Western Europe's energy situation. But the West German Government does what it can to smooth out whatever friction may arise between the United States and Western Europe. This is also the case with Western Germany's activities within NATO.

Last but not least, the Federal Republic with West Berlin play a key

A world-wide economic recession and dangers to the policy of détente led to frequent open-minded discussions between Chancellor Helmut Schmidt and President Gerald Ford in the White House

Chancellor Willy Brandt and President Richard M. Nixon, discussing the "new German Ostpolitik" in 1973

11

role in that undertaking to which the United States gives precedence: the search for achieving lasting, peaceful coexistence with the Soviet Union, despite continuing rivalry between the two superpowers. There have been no negotiations or agreements between Moscow and Washington which went beyond subjects of purely bilateral interest in which Germany has not been either a subject or object or in which Germany has not played an invisible role in the deliberations between the two superpowers. This has been the case ever since the very first of the many unsuccessful attempts to reestablish the unity of the German Nation were made. It also accompanied the establishment of full diplomatic relations between the United States and the German Democratic Republic (GDR) in the fall of 1974. And it continues throughout the present détente efforts.

And little will change in this respect in the future. The present situation in central Europe may be satisfactory to most foreign powers, but there is no doubt about its artificiality. It is impossible to predict whether the "German Problem" will remain a dormant issue for a long time to come or whether it may again suddenly become an object of dispute between East and West. But there is no question that the maintenance of the status quo in central Europe or its alteration by whatever developments imaginable would be unthinkable without the presence and participation of the United States. Therefore it can be expected that America's role in Germany will remain an active element of American foreign policy for many decades to come. Its purpose is to maintain the international balance of power, but in pursuing this goal Germany will of course take into consideration any political strategy worked out in Washington.

Any review of these German-American relations would be incomplete if it were not to consider also the basic changes which have taken place in Germany since 1945. It is not enough to speak of Germany and America only in terms of cooperation between Bonn and Washington. In the period of German sectionalism, the United States—from its founding in 1776 to the establishment of the German Reich in 1871 —maintained proper relations to the individual German states of Prussia, Hamburg, Bremen, Bavaria, Hannover and others. And today the United States again finds itself in the complex situation of having to deal with at least four German entities: first of all, there is the loyal ally, the Federal Republic of Germany. Then there is West Berlin, in which the United States and the other two powers (France and Great Britain) have special rights and responsibilities. In the camp of the communist nations of the Warsaw Pact there is the German Democratic Republic. And finally, there is the entity of Germany as a whole for which the USA and the three other powers bear special responsibilities based upon the occupation of 1945. Through the treaties of 1954 with the Federal Government the three Western Powers pledged their intention to pursue a policy of unification.

They still have these rights in Berlin despite the fact that they have not always been able to make use of them in the communist part of the city. It should be recalled that even though the Western Allies insist that there is to be no German military presence in greater Berlin, the National People's Army of the GDR often holds military parades in the eastern part of the city. The United States, France and Great Britain protest regularly and without success against these violations of the original postwar agreements on Berlin.

It is evident that the relations which the United States maintains to the Federal Republic of Germany have absolute priority in the many-faceted relationship which exists between America and "the Germans". And in this respect nothing will change as long as two German states are members of alliances in East and West which confront each other, and as long as Berlin remains a point of friction between them. There are, however, some symptoms of dynamic development in America's attitude and behavior toward the GDR though they are minimal. This development could be intensified if East Germany were to strive for more independence from its powerful Soviet protector. But at this stage the government in East Berlin does not appear to place any importance on this.

It is therefore most improbable that there will be a collision of American interests with those of Bonn and East Berlin. If this were to occur, America would without a doubt and without hesitation give priority to its relations with West Germany. Should, however, the GDR ever seek and acquire more independence and flexibility, then one could at least not exclude the possibility that this might tempt Washington to develop a more differentiated American policy toward "the two Germanys". As far-fetched as this may seem under the present circumstances it should not be discounted altogether.

The concept of the Federal Republic that devided Germany remains nevertheless indivisible as a nation which is still defended as a firm principle in the Federal Republic will hardly be perpetuated with the same fervor by the pragmatic Americans with their more detached views. To be sure, the communist government of the GDR itself can do much to keep the vision of a continuing "unity of the German Nation" alive in the minds of Americans. The goose-stepping of East German soldiers, for example, accomplishes precisely that while, simultaneously, keeping alive a negative image of "the Germans". At the same time, East Germany claims to be the cradle of such positive expressions of German intellect as Bert Brecht and Thomas Mann as ardently as Germans in the western part of the nation. But these are probably only temporary considerations. In all deliberations concerning the relationship between Germans and Americans it remains advisable to consider that from the present perspective the U.S. is after all, dealing with two very different societies and states on German soil. Washington will undoubtedly recognize this with much less constraint than what could be considered as conforming to the official standpoint of the Bonn government.

Paradoxically, the Germans themselves have yet to open their eyes to similar nuances in their observations of the American nation. Certainly, the United States has all of the pertinent markings of sovereignty, national unity, undisputed territorial indivisibility, internal democratic order and conformity of all of its ethnic and religious groups under a varnish coating of civilization. In those respects it is definitely a completely unified, homogeneous entity; indeed, the model specimen of the nation-state. However, just as much as the United States did not become divided or allow itself to be split into a "nation of nations", the American melting pot has not produced a standardized "typical" American.

Usually quite unconsciously, the average German bases his overall impression of America on that social class of Americans which indisputably dominates the social strata in America and whose members are of north and central European descent. The Germans account for the second largest number of immigrants, second only to those from Great Britain. It is therefore quite understandable that the image the average German has of the average American is that of one who belongs to the class from which—on the basis of its numerical size, its economic status and its large number of intellectual, political and military elite—America's leadership emerges.

But as America proceeds with the step-by-step and somewhat painful integration of other racial groupings (in the U.S. they are still quite revealingly referred to as "minorities" or "ethnics") into American society, America as a nation does begin to take on another coloring. One need only to consider the presence of about twenty-four million Afro-Americans, between seven and nine million "Chicanos" (American citizens of Mexican descent) as well as the large numbers of Puerto Ricans and Cubans. Then there are six million or more Jews and the strong Latin element inherent in the Italian, Spanish and South American immigrants and their offspring. Some characteristics traceable to the large numbers of East European immigrants are noticeable. The relatively small number of American Indians, quite aside from small sprinklings of Japanese, Chinese and — more recently — Vietnamese Americans also contribute to the American cultural landscape.

All of this is, of course, well known to Germans. But in general they have not become fully conscious of just how deep this heterogeneity of "Americans" goes. The average German still thinks of an American as a "Yankee" or—as he is described in present day colloquial German —as an "Ami". The German man-in-the-street views Americans with non-white or non-Anglo-Saxon backgrounds as an exotic addition to what they consider to be the true "American". He tends to overlook the significance of these non-Anglo-Saxons as indigenous factors of America, even though, for example, the Afro-American in reality and based solely on the numbers of generations his forefathers spent in "The New World" has even more claim to being called an "American" than most of the Caucasian immigrants and their offspring. Indeed, political-ethnic catchwords and slogans such as "black power" and "black is beautiful" have received an exceptionally strong resonance among politically interested and engaged German youth. But most Germans are not at all fully aware of either the social and political state of the non-Caucasian American and the "ethnic", the roles they play within American society or their attitudes toward America.

Without exaggeration, one can presume that the Germanization of America reached its climax with the large numbers of German immigrants in the nineteenth century. The Americanization of Germany, on the other hand, which could already be noticed during the Weimar Republic (1918—1933), began to culminate after 1945. One should differentiate between two distinct marks in this development. First of all, the German immigrant maintained the peculiarities of the German character and assumed the role of a "special element" in and of American society for only short periods during which they could be called "German-Americans". With but a few exceptions, the German immigrant never maintained double loyalties, and within the span of just a few generations felt himself to be a full-blooded American.

German and Americans share many basic qualities and traits. Both peoples have large organizational talent, are extremely productive, mobile and active; all characteristics which blend well with the realities of our industrialized age. They both have the capability for exploration in the modern, scientific age. Though as a result of their disastrous defeat in the second World War the Germans no longer claim that "the German soul shall save the world", the remarkable achievements of their "economic miracle" following this defeat have restored their secret pride and a certain tendency to believe that other countries need only to follow the German example of industriousness to have equal success. And, for their part, Americans believe that the rest of the world need merely adopt America's way of life in order to achieve greatness and happiness.

It would be almost ideal if one could unify the congruous positive characteristics of the Germans and Americans. We would like to quote an average citizen: a young American teacher of Dutch descent who —with open eyes and equal affection for both Germany and the United States — can make an impartial comparison. She teaches in Berlin and —something which is unusual for a female American citizen — has decided to stay in Germany. Her name is Nicoline Kokxhoorn. This young and intelligent lady earned her Bachelor of Arts degree in political science and French at Tufts University in Medford, Massachussetts and her Master's Degree in International Relations from Johns Hopkins School of Advanced International Studies in Washington, D.C., and at the school's branch in Bologna, Italy. As a sideline, she conducts scientific studies of international oil politics. She has worked for the Board of Education of West Berlin as an English teacher since April, 1971.

Ms. Kokxhoorn is convinced that she can enjoy all that is useful and good about the American way of life also in Germany. But, she points out, in Berlin and in West Germany she has the advantage of being able to escape from some of the unpleasant aspects of everyday life in America, such as crime in the street, the wretched rampancy of violence and brutality and the division of different social strata through geographical separation. She does not by any means like everything about the Germans, but, she says, she is impressed by the fact that in her new homeland contacts between people of varying social status today are much freer and more uninhibited than in the United States. For this reason, Ms. Kokxhoorn says, in all of her classes she tries to make her pupils aware of negative developments and social tensions in America. In her opinion, these could also become a problem in the Federal Republic of Germany, "a country which is basically not all too different from the United States". And, the American teacher adds: "As an American, I noticed immediately that there is no major difference—either in the political or economic systems—between the Federal Republic of Germany and the United States. Nevertheless, the special merits of the Federal Republic are that it is smaller, has a long tradition as a socially-oriented state and, in addition, is fortunate enough not to be a political world power."

"In my opinion", Ms. Kokxhoorn continues, "these three distinctions affect the individual German citizen in the following ways: in contrast to an American, the West German can obtain an overall general view of his country. This puts him in a position to know where what decisions are being made which affect his personal existence. So, a politically-minded citizen can more easily and more rewardingly be politically active because he has to concentrate on much fewer centers of power than an American. The fact that the Federal Republic of Germany is a socially-oriented state makes life here easier; here one can afford not to be healthy. Because the Federal Republic is not a world power, it is in a position to develop a balanced policy between East and West, it does not have to interfere in the internal affairs of other nations, above all not in those of developing countries. And so," Ms. Kokxhoorn concludes, "this fact and new forms of cooperation with these developing countries enables the Federal Republic to secure its supplies of essential raw materials."

We presented the quotations because they come from an unprejudiced American of the new generation who, after all, had five years in which to study her German surroundings. This made it possible for her to compare Germany with her own country on which, of course, she has no intention of turning her back.

As simple as it is today to diagnose the likenesses in the basic traits and characters of the American and German peoples, so it would be hazardous not to mention those insurmountable differences of national character which exist between the two nations. These are today more difficult to extract than in times past as a result of the high degree of interplay between Germany and the United States, which has been promoted quite consciously and has developed so quickly in almost all fields. Nevertheless, they cannot be overlooked and can easily be described.

The American is generally easygoing and carefree; the German is more often than not more pertinacious and cumbersome. The intellect of the American tends to be somewhat erratic, often superficial and oriented toward practical things; the German tends to be more contemplative, thorough and philosophical. The American acts as a realist with great feeling for what appeals to the majority; the German remains strongly romantic and tends to uncompromisingly take sides or to be eccentric. As a politically-interested person, the American concentrates mainly on temporary burning issues which he easily shakes off as soon as they have been solved; the German likes to think ideologically and is programmed toward a dramatic "Weltanschauung", a word for which there is none in English but which means basically world-outlook or philosphy of life. The American travels, so to speak, through the world of his existence without much baggage; the German usually chooses to bear a heavy burden. The American measures the world around him by dimensions in proportion to the large continent which he inhabits, with a king-size yardstick, and he intoxicates himself with the idea that there are quick and easy solutions to all problems; the German is accustomed to cramped surroundings and is therefore more hesitant, contemplative and inhibited in dealing with foreigners. This is why when abroad Germans try to conform as quickly as possible to their new surroundings; the American, on the other hand, is almost incapable of this assimilation and would much rather transplant a little piece of American (with schools, lawnmowers, supermarkets and ghetto-like compounds) to the country where he is staying.

As striking as it may sound to an American as a people, today's Germans have cast off those national traits so persistently attributed to them: they rarely display their flag, only reluctantly do they sing their national anthem, they have no desire to display their power and no longer want to rule anyone else. If but given the chance, they would be only too glad to be fully incorporated into a unified Europe. The picture which the American presents of himself abroad, however, is that of the classic nationalist: in elementary school his children pledge allegiance to the flag every day, the American flag and the national anthem are ever present, and the American still maintains that the United States produces the largest, newest and most beautiful things in the world.

The older German may still show the effect of the centuries-long pounding into him that he must believe and have faith in the authority and other powers; but lately, because of the experience of the Hitler years, he has become more sceptical and wary. The American has mixed feelings about government. On one hand, because of the disturbing events of recent years, he views his federal government with deep distrust and on the other has tended to almost destructiv self-criticism. This has brought about a discernible detachment between the Citizen and the State.

Let us wrap up this compact survey of similarities and differences between Germans and Americans, but not without drawing at least a few significant conclusions: The United States of America and the Federal Republic of Germany are countries which are far distant from each other not only geographically, but also in their intellectual structures, their national traits and characteristics, their behavior and in their objectives. The more they recognize and are aware of these differences, the more able they will be to avoid misunderstandings and conflicts.

2

The New World –
a magnet for Germans

The Germans did not discover America, but they christened it. In fact, the German geographer and cartographer Martin Waldseemueller gave the "New World" the name it has had ever since.

As a member of a circle of scholars in St. Dié in Lothringen, he was commissioned at the beginning of the 16th century by Duke Renatus II to make a cosmographic survey of the world on the basis of a report on Italian seafarer Amerigo Vespucci's voyages to what we know today as South and Central America. In this "Cosmographiae Introductio" (which was written in Latin, the language used by scholars of those days), Waldseemueller made the following proposals:

"But now these parts of the 'Old World' have also been explored more thoroughly and another, fourth part has been discovered by Amerigo Vespucci... I do not see why one should not quite rightfully name this part after its discoverer, Amerigo, a man of great discernment, and call it 'Amerigo's Land' or 'A m e r i c a'. Its geographical location and the customs of its people are described in great detail in Amerigo's following four voyages."

It is believed that at approximately the same time he wrote these words, Waldseemueller designed a globe consisting of twelve segments on which the strangely depicted "New World" was referred to as "America". In this epoch of great discoveries by Spaniards, Portuguese, Italians, Englishmen and Dutchmen, all news from far away lands was eagerly devoured in Europe. And with the invention of printing in Germany by Johannes Gutenberg, the news made the rounds even faster than before. "America", the name recommended by Waldseemueller, started coming more and more into use.

Christopher Columbus himself was partially and indirectly responsible for this turn of events. On October 12, 1492, he became the first European to set foot on the Caribbean island of Guanahani. But in contrast to Vespucci, who sought notoriety, Columbus took pains to keep the travel reports he sent to the Spanish Courts as confidential as possible. Moreover, Columbus initially did not know exactly what he had discovered. Thus, Waldseemueller herad about Columbus' voyages much later than those of Vespucci. He then went about correcting his error and even credited Columbus with the discovery of the "New World" on a new map he drew up in 1513. But the name "America" had already become a label which could not easily be erased. Soon, fascination with the newly-discovered part of the world began to have a magnetic effect on the Germans.

As legend has it, a German named "Tyrker" was along on the Leif Ericson expedition which is supposed to have landed in North America around the year 1000. But we must accept the fact that this brave fellow "Tyrker" did not leave behind any traces we are aware of today. The Germans, therefore, can quietly sit back and leave the age-old controversy over who discovered America to the other countries which make this claim.

In any case, Germans had no part in the first settlements in Florida by the Spaniards or the British and Dutch settlements in New England and farther down the East Coast; at least there is no mention of German participation in the history books. But the Germans did play a considerable role in spreading knowledge about the newly-discovered land to the old continent. At that time Germans were the leading printers, geographers, authors and cartographers in Europe. For this reason it should be mentioned specifically that cosmographer Johann Ruysch, printer Jobst Ruchamen and author Johannes Schoenberger, all Germans, made decisive contributions to making the first facts about America known to a large public.

As the other Europeans discovered and began to explore the huge territories of North, Central and South America between the end of the 15th and the middle of the 17th centuries, the Germans soon felt themselves drawn to the "New World" by a completely different motive than the mere thrill of discovery: The Germans were interested in trade and profit.

The first Germans to enter the scene with this motivation were members of the merchant House of Welser. Together with the even more significant German merchant Fugger Family, the Welsers paid the bribes which helped Spanish King Karl I ("on whose realm the sun never set") to be elected German Emperor Karl V. In return, the merchant House of Welser became the first German trading firm to be given the privilege of trading in the new territories. Until then, 1525, only Spaniards enjoyed these rights. And soon these rights were granted by Spain to all Germans.

The central point of what had been discovered of the "American World" was Santo Domingo (the larger part of "Hispaniola", the rest of which is Haiti). Soon, the German merchants built their first trading vessels for doing business with Santo Domingo. The island trading center was then the Spanish city of Sevilla.

On behalf of the Welsers, Hieronimus Sailer concluded a contract in 1528 hiring fifty German miners from the Erz Mountains. They arrived in Santo Domingo and began to dig for copper and gold on the island. Another contract dated February 12, 1528, gave the Welsers the approval of the Spanish Crown to transport four thousand African workers to Santo Domingo. New workers were needed because the Indian natives had either already become the victims of their association with the white discoverers or had fled inland to avoid exploitation and possible death. These German merchants were neither the first nor the last Europeans to bring black Africans to newly-discovered America as slaves. And ironically enough, later on in history it was Americans of German descent who fought ferociously for the abolition of slavery in the United States.

It is extremely difficult to determine exactly where or when Germans first settled in North America. There are only seldom mentioned —if at all—in the chronicles which tell the story of the beginnings of the settlement of the "New World". But the date registered by history is the day on which the influx of German Mennonites landed with their families in Philadelphia aboard the "Concorde". They were weavers from Krefeld, a West German city which to this very day still maintains a long tradition as a cloth weaving center. The ship which brought what is believed were the first German settlers to America was jokingly referred to in the annals as "the German Mayflower". This first group of German immigrants on record soon founded their own settlement near Philadelphia. And they named it "Germantown".

It may well be the intent of every author who concerns himself with the history of America to view the role which his own nationality played in the rise of this hitherto unknown continent under a magnifying glass and to over-exaggerate its importance to the development of North America. We, however, shall attempt to resist this temptation.

Indeed, until the outbreak of World War I, the Germans accounted for the second largest group of immigrants, second only to the immigrants from the British Isles (English, Welsh, Scots), even outnumbering the Irish. There were times in American history in which Germans made up one third of the population of some large states and had "Germanized" entire regions with their own schools, clubs and newspapers. And for a span of American history there were even periodic attempts to establish one or more autonomous German states. But despite all of these facts, there was never a serious political attempt to put a German stamp on America.

The conflicts between the early settlers (the English, Spanish, French and Dutch), the decline of Spain as a world power and the rise of Great Britain to ruling the waves gave the population of the British

Isles the upper hand in influencing developments in the "New World". And it was not long before their language, culture and their judicial system were impressed upon the thirteen colonies from which the United States was to emerge as a result of the War of Independence. The Germans with few exceptions were completely absorbed as if through catalysis into the American nation via this Anglo-Saxon element.

The protracted and sometimes bitter rivalries between the immigrants of different nationalities prompted some of them to claim for themselves a sort of primogeniture, or the rights of the firstborn in shaping young America. Since in the many intervals of history the one side was up and the other down or the one side was down and the other up, it was unavoidable that historic accounts of which nationality made what contribution toward developing the United States should be distorted and subjective. For this reason there are accounts in which the contribution made by the Germans is minimized or falsified and the others in which their role seems to be exaggerated and magnified. The events which occured between 1914 and 1918 and between 1933 and 1945, for example, were especially well-suited to bring about the discreditation or disavowal of Germans in the United States and the part they played as an ethnic group in building America.

It is not the object of the author or the purpose of his writing to correct or to rehabilitate. And there is no question whatsoever that the Germans neither discovered, conquered nor built America. But there is also no denying that together with other nationalities they did, indeed, play a foremost part in the development and formation of America. What distinguishes them from some of the other founding peoples is that the Germans were quicker to shed their nationality and to grow an American skin. They were quick to merge not because there was any reason to be ashamed of their origin but simply (and perhaps inexplicably) because Germans have tended to do this abroad all throughout history with some exceptions in Eastern Europe and South America.

The development and settlement of North America — primarily through energetic colonization by the British — was most pronounced in the middle of the 17th century; at a time when Germany was in its most desolate situation since the Middle Ages. Germany lay waste; farmers and artisans were hungry for both bread and work; even mercenaries were unemployed. No wonder then, that many Germans longed for a secure spot where they would be spared the consequences of war, religious intolerance and the economic exploitation and political suppression by their titled masters. But at that time a new continent such as "America" was far from the thoughts of the average

German. Most Germans lacking education probably did not even know the name of the place.

And this remained the case for several decades, until the bustling and enterprising British made the Germans aware of the new wonderland and encouraged them to shake off the dust of their fatherland and to push off on their way across the Atlantic to America. At the beginning of the 18th century, English promoters traveled up and down the Rhineland and through southern Germany promising the Germans heaven on earth if they would pack up and move "over there". Quite often these agents painted the rosiest pictures of the freedom and opportunities for social advancement awaiting German immigrants in America.

But since most Germans who at that time were interested in emigrating were hardly in a position to pay for their own transportation, many of them—just as their fellow-sufferers from other countries— had no choice but to sign contracts obligating themselves to serve their English masters in America as servants, maids or handymen for between three and seven years. By signing on the dotted line, however, they put themselves into semi-bondage and soon discovered, much to their horror, that they had sold their souls not for three or seven but often for ten, twenty or thirty years. In addition, thousands of men, women and children never reached the promised land: they died, herded together in mass quarters aboard swimming coffins, poorly-fed and often the victims of many months on stormy seas without proper nutrition or medical care. Many an immigrant who set sail for the "New World" never set foot on the coast of America. Nevertheless and despite news of such trials and tribulations, indefatigable Germans, motivated by want, were not discouraged from risking their lives for the sake of a new life in the new world.

The year 1709 can be considered the beginning of the mass emigration of Germans to America. It was in this year that about twelve thousand Germans crowded aboard ships in British harbors. And as miserable as the voyages and possibilities for getting a new start in the new land may have been, for some of these brave immigrants and their offspring, America turned out after all to be the land of unlimited opportunities, economic prosperity and religious freedom.

The Germans had varying motives for emigrating from their homeland to America. But there were some predominating reasons: First of all, the German tribes had always had a lively roving spirit. One need only to recall their movements during the era of Migration of Nations. For a long time Germans were on the move as colonizers, as participants in crusades and as mercenaries in foreign countries, just as tourists every year have found a more friendly outlet for their wanderlust. Germans cross their own borders in greater numbers every year than any other European people, and millions of them now stream into Italy, France, Spain or Greece and Yougoslavia.

This yearning for far-away places and social, economic and professional motivations are primarily responsible for the German emigration to America. And the identity of character which exists between the Germans and large segments of the American people only underlines the significance of this yearning. The differences in the language and way of living between the two peoples were slight and easily surmountable.

The first German settlements in the USA in the 18th and 19th centuries were the centers where new arrivals could get a foothold on the new continent. But today the degree of conformity in the civilizations of the two countries is so high that a German immigrant is no longer confronted with the same initial difficulties which hardly a century ago forced him to cling to his former countrymen in his new surroundings.

The second motivation for emigration was a yearning for political and religious freedom. This was the case with some groups and religous sects as well as the "Forty-eighters", who were politically very prominent. They were Germans who were persecuted in their homeland following the collapse of the revolution of 1848—49. It was also the motivation for the German Jews who were forced to wait for emancipation and equality until late in the 19th century. And this certainly was the case with the German Jews who were the object of Adolf Hitler's racist insanity and the political dissidents who refused to conform to Nazi policies.

But measured solely on the basis of numbers, all of these groups motivated to emigrate by wanderlust and for religious or political reasons make up a minority. The large majority of Germans who went to America went for purely social and economic reasons. They immigrated to the new continent in search of a better way of life and nothing else. In America they worked hard, were productive and were quick to adapt to their new surroundings.

Nevertheless, most outstanding and well-known German-Americans had their origins in the circles of immigrants who came to America for intellectual rather than economic reasons. Their intellects could unfold more freely once they had fled the narrow political and religious confines of their homeland. And the freedom which they found in the United States was especially conducive to intellectual creativity. In addition, many German scientists, technicians and artists found better material conditions for creative development in America. Between the two World Wars and after 1945, this cost Germany much talent to the benefit of the US. These conclusions can be drawn from data available on the extent, composition and periodicity of overall German emigration to America.

Since reliable statistics on German immigration are to be obtained almost exclusively from American sources (and only precisely since 1820), the following data and analyses are based almost without exception on official publications put out by the US Department of Justice's Immigration and Naturalization Service and the Department of Commerce's Bureau fo the Census. And for our purposes we have rounded off and simplified the figures.

First of all, some fundamental facts concerning the subject of immigration to America should be mentioned. In the past centuries and (with only occasional, minor exceptions) up to the present, the United States has pursued the most liberal and open immigration policy in the world. But Washington drew a careful line (motivated by ethnic and political considerations) restricting this immigration to the white, caucasian countries of the northern hemisphere while occasionally giving preference to the central and north European peoples and to Canada. The "colored" continents of Africa and Asia have been excluded almost to the point of being barred altogether. The most significant exception was the Afro-Americans (now accounting for about twelve per cent of the total population, or 24 million people), whose forefathers, however, did not come to the new world of their own free will but were abducted to America as slaves.

The most pronounced example of this preference for persons of European origin in America's stratified immigration legislation is the law of 1924, in which the annual quota for each nationality group was based on the number of persons of the same origin already in the United States in 1920. This "quota system" was replaced in 1965 by a law which set the annual quota for immigrants on a world-wide basis. This new law went into effect on July 1, 1968.

This law, which is in effect to this day, contains a decisive provision giving the American government authority to regulate the stream of immigrants. The law stipulates that a maximum of 170,000 immigrants can enter the United States yearly and that issuance of an immigration visa depends on whether or not the Secretary of Labor certifies that the newcomer has a profession which is needed in the United States. So, this means that legal immigration into the United States is now clearly restricted to people with certain professional qualifications. And trained people can be expected to come almost exclusively from countries of the northern hemisphere and, to a smaller degree, from Latin America.

America's naturalization laws have always been as liberal as its immigration laws. The regulations governing naturalization stipulate that citizenship shall be granted to the applicant once he or she has been in the United States for five years, during which the person in question has respected the country's laws and has familiarized himself with the Constitution and has made a formal declaration of intention. Consequently, the immigration and naturalization policies of the United States have always been especially advantageous to the Germans and other Europeans. The exceptions, of course, have been in times when Germany and America have been at war with each other and in the periods immediately following these conflicts.

America's period of immigration came in three or four great waves during the 19th century and in the first three decades of the 20th century. These waves were, of course, in addition to the early settlement and colonization of America by the British, which we shall leave aside for simplicity's sake.

The most thorough American statisticians cannot determine with certainty the national origins of all America's present day citizens. Many Americans cannot specify their origins either because their ancestry consists of several nationalities or because they simply are not aware of their extraction. However, according to a survey made in 1972, there is no doubt that persons of German extraction make up the second largest group of Americans whose ethnic origins can be determined, second only to the descendants of immigrants from the British Isles (English, Scot and Welsh). It should be noted that this was ascertained on the basis of answers given by persons polled in the 1972 survey and not based on second-hand information.

In that survey of America's 204.8 million citizens it was determined that the ancestors of 102.2 million of them belonged to eight ethnic categories of immigrants: British, Irish, German, Italian, French, Polish, Russian and Spanish. Among them the five largest specific ethnic origin groups were as follows:

English, Scot, or Welsh	29.5 million persons
German	25.5 million persons
Irish	16.4 million persons
Spanish	9.2 million persons
Italian	8.8 million persons

On the basis of traceable ancestry, Americans of German origin therefore account for between twelve and thirteen per cent of the population of the United States in the bicentennial year. The wide-spread belief that every sixth American (or nearly seventeen per cent of the total population) has German forefathers is without official statistical foundation, at least there is no mathematical proof of this.

Presumably, only every seventh or eight American is of German ancestry.

Since immigration in the 17th and 18th centuries was relatively small (in 1790 the population of the United States was a mere 3.93 million), one need only to look at the statistics of the 19th and 20th centuries to comprehend the social composition as well as the reasons for the fluctuations in the flow of German immigrants to America. In the aftermath of the Napoleonic Wars between 1820 and 1838 the flow was but a trickle. In 1832, for example, only 148 German immigrants were registered in America. The highest number recorded in these two decades was 23,740. That was in 1837. But then the number begins to climb. In 1849, for instance, there were more than 60,000. The number of German immigrants passed the 100,000 mark in 1852, when approximately 146,000 landed in America.

A real "German immigrant boom" can be registered between 1866 and 1873, the period in which the German Reich was founded on blood and iron. In the course of these eight years, more than a million Germans set sail for America. German immigration reached its absolute peak between 1880 and 1892, when 1.77 Million Germans arrived in the "New World". 1882 was the highest single year with a quarter of a million. The beginning of the 20th century saw a gradual drop in this "German curve" and shortly before the second world war climbed back to a yearly average of between 20,000 and 30,000 immigrants.

The war brought a pause. In 1919, only 52 Germans were let into the United States. But between 1923 and 1930 the flow began to pick up again and between 26,000 and 75,000 German immigrants per year were registered. World War II brought about a similar decline to the point at which in 1945 only 172 Germans immigrated to the United States of America. But soon after the war the gates were opened to Germans once again, then on the basis of the new quota system. After the system was abolished the gates were opened wide.

Between 1945 and 1973, a total of 924,000 Germans took advantage of the opportunity to immigrate to the United States. The peak of this new wave was reached with 128,000 immigrants in 1950, almost all of them coming from West Germany. And as the "German economic miracle" became more and more stable, the number of Germans who emigrated to America became less and less. This has been the trend since 1969 and has now dropped to an average of between six and seven thousand persons per year.

The unexpected climax between 1947 and 1957 was attributable to more than merely the poor economic condition of postwar Germany. It also had a very human and heart-moving reason: the loneliness felt by thousands of young American GI's stationed far away from home in the Federal Republic of Germany. Nature took its course and it was quite natural for many of them to chose German women for their wives. In fact, in all of history there never were as many marriages performed between German girls and women and young American soldiers as in the years since 1945.

In many of the thirty years which lie between the end of World War II and the American bicentennial, official records show three times as many female as male Germans emigrating to the United States. According to statistics, between 1945 and 1975 American men married about 135,000 women from West Germany and West Berlin. The Arm Chief Chaplain yestimates that the number is probably even higher. The large number (which is considerably higher than those for Italian, Japanese and English women) can be explained by the particularly large number of American troops stationed in West Germany and West Berlin.

Whereas the Germans who came to America in the 17th century primarily in search of religious freedom had settled for the most part in Pennsylvania ("Pennsylvania Dutch"), Delaware and in the Carolinas, the immigrants who followed them grew new roots along the entire East Coast, in the North West and above all in the Middle West, mainly in Illinois and Wisconsin. In addition to religious intolerance and political oppression, the reasons for their emigration were also economic: the uprooting of the rural population by the beginnings of the Industrial Revolution, periodic economic crises and poor potato and wheat harvests (both important food staples in Germany).

The mass-emigrations which took place after the middle of the 19th century (a time in which Germany experienced increasing liberalization, the founding of the German Reich, the loss of most privileges for German nobility and more religious coexistence) were no longer undertaken primarily for political reasons. This movement was not motivated by a need to flee. Of the estimated seven to eight million Germans who found a new home in America between 1600 and 1975, the great majority was driven to the foreign shore by economic necessity or was drawn there by the magnetism of the land of unlimited opportunities. Whoever compares the waves of German emigration with Germany's economic history will immediately recognize the direct connection between the two developments.

The more similar the standards of living and ways of life of the two nations become (the average income of Germans living in the Federal Republic is now almost the same as that of the average American), the more emigration becomes a two-way process. This is evident by the fact that between 1953 and 1973, more than 160,000 Germans moved back to Germany from America. This reverse-emigration process had also taken place in similar numbers (about 18 per cent of the German immigrants) in the years between 1908 and 1924. And since the end of the second World War more Americans have made their homes in Germany than at any other time in history.

According to the figure of the West German Federal Bureau of Statistics, more than 72,000 civilian American citizens now reside in West Germany and West Berlin. Of these, about 15,000 are employed by German industry, work in other areas of trade and in the banking or insurance business. This is mainly the result of substantial holding by American capital in German companies and increasing American ownership of German firms. A few Americans have been prompted by reasons of nostalgia to settle in Germany, most of them artists and musicians. The number of Americans who apply for German citizenship is now only two to three hundred per year.

Nevertheless, it should be pointed out that in the thirty years since 1945 in which West Germany was either an occupied or allied country, the number of Americans who made either temporary or permanent homes in Germany for personal of professional reasons was higher than during any other period of history. And this is not counting the 37,000 calling cards which GI's left behind in the form of illegitimate children. The question of who should pay for their support has often been the object of long and unfruitful disputes.

The seven to eight million Germans who emigrated to America were (at least up to the middle of the 19th century) mainly farmers, handymen and unskilled workers. There were also large numbers of persons from the "educated classes", soldiers and plain adventurers. The latter usually embarked to America at the urging of parents who wanted their "lost son" to build a spotless existence in the "New World". With the coming of industrialization, the number of skilled workers from the metal and mining industries who emigrated to America began to increase. And the number of merchants, scientists, engineers and artists who were enticed to try their luck in the land of unlimited opportunity also rose.

Today, most Americans of German descent can be found in America's large "middle class". In the real dominating "elite class" of a nation (members of government, the military, higher institutions of learning, the management of large businesses, the world of high finance and the national associations and labor unions), the German element can be found in America most predominantly in the military, the universities and in some branches of business. Anglo-Saxons and Americans of Irish, Italian and Russian descent are much more visibly predominant in the other spheres of American society's "elite class".

Just as most immigrant groups (with the exception of the British), the Germans had to make their places in America in tough competition with other ethnic groups. But rivalries and disputes with Americans of other ethnic origins disappeared with the almost total amalgamation of the German element with American society. Even during both World Wars the Germans in America were never "persecuted" as an ethnic group (as was the fate of the Japanese), though some of the German traits or imported traditions and habits sometimes were defamed. This was the case especially during the first World War. Between 1914 and 1918, pro British American newspapers actually went so far as to campaign for changing the name of sauerkraut to "liberty cabbage"!

The original focal points of geographic settlement by German-Americans still remain, but now they are not as pronounced as they were in the last century. All in all, the distribution of Americans of German descent corresponds with that of the American public in general, even though the Germans still have a marked preference for large East Coast cities, the Middle West, California, Texas and the states in the south eastern sections of the United States.

As far as income is concerned, the German-American can be found toward the center of the scale; slightly above the average national income but below the average income of some other ethnic groups. In 1972, the average yearly income of male German-Americans above fourteen years of age was $ 7,693 and of females $ 2,510. The average income of a German-American family was $ 10,977, which put this ethnic group ahead of the Americans of French and Spanish origins but behind the Russian, Polish, Italian, British and Irish Americans. But all in all the differences were not substantial. The average income of a Russian-American family, for instance, was $ 13,929 and that of the Spanish-American family $ 7,595.

In 1972, German-Americans were proportionately employed in the following categories:

Prof., tech.	15.0 %
Managers and administrators, except farm	13.9 %
Sales	7.0 %
Clerical	6.0 %
Craftsmen	21.7 %
Operatives, including transport	16.5 %
Laborers, except farm	5.2 %
Farmers and farm managers	5.9 %
Farm laborers and farm foremen	2.0 %
Service workers, except private household	6.7 %
Private household	0.1 %
	100.0 %

In this respect, Americans of Russian descent also top the proportionate number of German-Americans in "higher-up jobs", as do the Italians and British. The overall picture of the present-day German-American shows that he has now been able to establish himself firmly in the white collar jobs, whereas during the epochs of mass-immigration he was predominently a blue collar worker.

3
Small People
and big Achievements

Whoever moves to a far distant country as an emigrant undertakes the journey with completely different feelings than a tourist who is only after new impressions or experiences. The immigrant wants to create a new existence for himself in new surroundings, but is not so sure he will be able to adapt to them so easily. The tourist risks having good or bad experiences, but in the back of his mind has the feeling that he will eventually return home. The immigrant, however, has burned his bridges behind him and must—for better or for worse—make do with what he finds in his new homeland.

Most immigrants go through tremendous inner conflicts during the first stage of their presence in the new surroundings. And no one described better the doubts which arose than one of the outstanding "Forty-Eighter", Carl Schurz. He was the most prominent German-American of the 19th century and eventually became a United States Senator and Secretary of the Interior. In his memoirs, he writes how the new impressions cause him inner conflicts and how he eventually overcomes them. Immediately after arriving in New York on September 17, 1852 (when his wife suddenly took ill), he first encountered that American readiness to help which, he writes, "was then (and I firmly believe still is today) one of the most beautiful and characteristic traits of this people."

Schurz was captivated by the beauty of the countryside and gasped at "... the serious and thoughtful faces of the old and young men moving about so sprightly; the women, some of whom are dressed in striking, brightly-colored clothing, bustling about their business with such understanding expressions on their faces; the surprising similarity of the people, both in their expressions and facial characteristics as well as their attire, even though they surely belong to different classes of society." Indeed, Carl Schurz had the same initial impression of Americans as millions of other German immigrants probably had before and after him.

But many an evening, Schurz sat in a park near New York's Union Square trying to organize the impressions which overwhelmed him. "These hours", he later wrote, "were among the most melancholy of my life. There I was in the great Republic, the goal of my dreams, feeling so totally alone and forlorn. The future seemed to hover before me wrapped in an impenetrable cloud. What I had seen was not so very different from Europe—as I had expected it to be—, but nevertheless so strange and mysterious. Would my experiences here be able to translate into reality that ideal which I had imagined, or would they destroy it? I had to struggle hard against this gloomy brooding. But finally I was able to convince myself that in order to get in step with the hectic life around me, I would have to become active myself; would have to become a part of it—and the sooner the better."

Carl Schurz, the most prominent liberal "Forty-eighter" from Germany, who became US Secretary of the Interior and was a friend of Abraham Lincoln

In these few sentences, Schurz had sketched the three basic stages which the emigrant from Germany went through in the New World. At first, his attitude toward America was ambivalent; the country held much promise for him but some things repelled him. For a while, he was overcome by a feeling of insecurity. Then, he recognized the dynamic nature of this environment challenging him to action. And finally, he became a part of it simply in order to be able to survive in its midst.

And this is precisely how—consciously or unconsciously—the greater part of the Germans in America acted. The initial German settlers didn't have much time to think about it; just as the immigrants from other countries, they had to wage their battle for existence with a rich but as yet undeveloped and therefore hostile open country. This became less difficult once the United States of America was founded and industrialization began to change the country. But even today, the newcomer to America finds himself without much special help in getting a start. Self-help and neighborly assistance were, and still are the prerequisites for getting a foothold for survival and for advancement.

But despite all of these hardships, the German emigrant was driven to America by what were primarily optimistic expectations. Whether in popular novels or in serious and well-researched reports, German literature has dealt with America more as the Land of Promise rather than with those aspects of the New World which might repel the reader. A short poem consisting of only three verses written by the prince of German poets, Johann Wolfgang von Goethe (who never set foot in the New World himself), summed it up for all time in the first line: "America, your lot is fairer . . ."

It was also Goethe—following talks in 1827 with German scholar Alexander von Humboldt—who foresaw America's future. With a prophetic eye on a country completely unknown to him personally, Goethe wrote the following:

"It can be predicted that in thirty or forty years, this youthfoul country will have also taken possession of and populated the huge territories on the other side of the Rocky Mountains. It can also be predicted that along the entire coast of the Pacific Ocean, where nature has already provided the most spacious and secure harbors, significant trading cities will gradually emerge in order to accomodate great traffic between China and East India and the United States. In such a case, however, it would not only be desireable but also imperative that trading vessels as well as war ships maintain faster connections between North America's western and eastern coasts than has been possible up to now with

the boring, unpleasant and expensive journey around Cape Horn. So, I repeat, "Goethe concluded," it is completely essential for the United States to create a throughway from the Gulf of Mexico to the Pacific Ocean, and I am sure that it will accomplish this."

Goethe did not live to see or hear about either San Francisco, San Diego or even the Panama Canal. But his predictions do not only testify to great acumen; they are an expression of the burning interest which so many Germans had in the new, young nation. Of course, not many Germans read all of what Goethe had to say about America. Most of them even today get their initial impressions of America from entirely different authors; from James F. Cooper's "Leatherstocking Tales", from Harriet Beecher-Stowe, who gained rapid fame in Germany with "Uncle Tom's Cabin", or—since the end of the 19th century—from the pen of a German ex-convict who had never even been in America when he wrote his numerous novels set in the New World. It was Karl May who, with the adventures of his fictitious characters of Winnetou and Old Shatterhand, since 1893 has provided several generations of young Germans with more cliché conceptions of America than any western novel could ever have accomplished. Karl May, the most widely-read German author of all times (more than fifty million copies sold), did more to romanticize the clash between the white and the red man, and thereby America, in the minds of Germany's youth than even any German author who knew America first-hand.

But more important than the shaping and then temporary paling of the Germans' concept of America was the part German immigrants played in the development of their new homeland. After all, they had to survive in a raw, realistic world and not in the pages of an idealistic novel. One can measure by their overall success what the German immigrants gave to America and what America gave to them. History was written in the past recording the deeds of heroes, dynasties and battles. In our times, however, history is written with more attention paid to sociological developments and interplay between social classes. In our presentation, we can neither ignore the German—American "heroes" nor the simple, anonymous man. The "heroes" are the exponents of large groups, with the one reflecting the story of the others.

For example, though the Declaration of Independence was not decided or formulated by Americans of German extraction, it was a German-language newspaper in America, the "Pennsylvania Staatsbote" which on July 5, 1776 was the first newspaper in the entire country to publish (in the antiquated German of those times) the news of this proclamation:

"Philadelphia, den 5. July. Gestern hat der Achtbare Congress

dieses Vesten Landes die Vereinigten Colonien Freye und Unab-
hängige Staaten erkläret.
Die Declaration in Englisch ist jetzt in der Presse; sie ist datiert
den 4ten July, 1776, und wird heut oder morgen im druck erschei-
nen."
Translation: "Philadelphia, the 5th of July. Yesterday the Most
Honourable Congress of this continental country proclaimed the
United Colonies to be Free and Independent States. The Decla-
ration in Englisch is being put into print, it is dated July 4th, 1776
and shall appear in print either today or tomorrow."

Soon thereafter the Germans demonstrated their love of freedom as Americans in the battles of the War of Independence. Instances such as this illustrated how the Germans moved with the tide of developments in America. Sometimes they were the cause of the developments, sometimes they only participated passively. But the German immigrants were never separated from the development of their new homeland, regardless of what social strata they belonged to.

Large numbers of the first German immigrants were of Protestant denomination or religious sects such as Pietists, Mennonites, the followers of Kaspar Schwenkfeld, Quakers or Amish. The number of Catholics among the immigrants was almost as high as that of the Protestants; both denominations were driven to the New World in search of more freedom to practice their religion. The German clergymen of all of these confessions were therefore naturally responsible for much of the creative development in the Protestant and Catholic churches of America.

The rivalry which existed between the Catholics of German origin and the Irish Catholics, who controlled the hierarchy of that church for a long time in America, provided for much lively religious fervor. And to this very day, theologians of German extraction have exercised considerable influence on both confessions in America. One need only think of leading Protestants such as Paul Tillich and Reinhold Niebuhr or Catholic Father Theodore Hesburg, President of Notre Dame University, George Nauman Shuster, who was President of Hunter College in New York and co-founder of the Catholic weekly "Commonweal" as well as Elmer Cardinal Ritter. Niebuhr, who died in 1971, also influenced politics in America as a progressive liberal. He supported the "Americans for Democratic Action" (ADA) and was celebrated as the guardian angel of intellectual freedom in an environment which tended more and more to be determined by technology.

Germans were among the city fathers of many American municipalities, since the early immigrants tended to cluster together in settlements restricted to people of the same religion or origins. It was their descendants who first spread out over the entire country and by inter-marriage eventually erased the families' national origins. One of the first to cut the umbilical cord was lawyer Franz Daniel Pastorius who founded Germantown near Philadelphia in 1683. The map of the United States is heavily sprinkled with German names which clearly reveal the origin of their first inhabitants: Berlin, Stuttgart, Francfort, Bismarck, Fredericksburg, New Braunfels, etc.

Road sign in Arkansas, illustrating German origin of many American cities

And many landmarks also have a German history. Acting on the part of Holland, German Peter Minnewit (later "Minuit"), who immigrated in 1626, purchased Manhattan for sixty guilders from the Indians. Later he built a fortress at the tip of this island which became known as "The Battery" a name it still bears. The Brooklyn Bridge is the creation of German immigrant architect, John Roebling, and his son. Historic Harpers Ferry, still a magnet for many tourists, was built by German immigrant Robert Harper. The grandiose design for Washington, D. C., is the work of the French engineer, Officer Pierre L'Enfant, but public buildings in the nation's capital and some of its schools were built by Adolph Cluss, now a forgotten name. Many of these schools are still today considered exemplary because of their spaciousness and hygienic and pedagogic standards. It may be of interest that Cluss was an intellectual associate of Karl Marx. But the greatest influence of German architectural talent on America was exerted by Germans who were forced to emigrate by Hitler: names such as Walter Gropius (who later became Director of the Harvard University Department of Architecture) and Mies van der Rohe are cases in point.

The influence of German music on America, particularly in the 19th century, is undisputed. This ranges from popular drinking songs (which led to the introduction of the country fair and even the "Octoberfest" in the United States) to the great classical composers Bach, Beethoven, Brahms and Wagner. The Italians rule the opera, but German composers dominate America's concert halls.

Interplay between Germany and the United States in the field of literature is especially pronounced. This goes far beyond common knowledge of works which are considered part of world literature and therefore receive international distribution anyway. American authors of political science, modern history, sociology and psychology are high up on the list of foreign authors who are read in West Germany. Numerous novelists and dramatists, from Sinclair Lewis and Ernest Hemingway to Thornton Wilder and James Baldwin, have captured the hearts of German readers and theatergoers. German classic authors and their successors were widely read in the United States, especially in the 19th and 20th centuries. Thomas Mann, Stefan Zweig, Bert Brecht, Erich Maria Remarque ("All Quiet on the Western front") and Carl Zuckmayer took their places in America's reading repertoire before and during their emigration to America. And Hermann Hesse ("Steppenwolf") experienced a real renaissance during the nostalgia wave of the 1970's.

The roots of this intensive intellectual communication reach all the way back to the first decades of German immigration. In Europe they were brought to life by the manifold ties between various German and English religious reformers, of whom some belonged to the first settlers in America. Next to literature of English origin, in the colonies literature from the pens of Germans—some in German, some in Latin—was in first place, especialy in the fields of geography, astronomy, political theory and linguistics. One of the leading men in the colonies, John Winthrop Jr., who became founder and the first Governor of Connecticut in 1657, made himself a promoter of German intellectualism in America. He maintained comprehensive correspondence with German scientists and stocked his private library (for those times an enormous collection of about one thousand books) with numerous works by German authors.

And it was barely a century later that Benjamin Franklin showed great interest in the German intellect and in spreading its fruits. He printed German catechisms, songbooks, prayer books and text books and apparently even some editions of the first German news-paper in America, the "Philadelphische Zeitung". While on a trip to Europe in 1776, he visited one of the leading universities of that time, the University of Göttingen. Much later, higher education in historical sciences as had been developed first in the famous "Historisches Seminar" of this German university were adopted in America at Johns Hopkins University. It set an example for the development of graduate courses in other institutions of higher education.

These are just a few examples of German—American intellectual interaction selected at random. Of even greater importance is the overall influence of German pedagogics on America. Some experts believe that the introduction of compulsory education and the system of public schools instituted by the states in America was mainly the result of German influence. And America's efforts to steer the pre-school development of children were heavily influenced by the ideas of German educators, such as Friedrich Froebel. In fact, the German word "Kindergarten" was simply taken over in America's vocabulary. Frau Schurz, the wife of the famous "Forty-Eighter", is supposed to have founded the first American kindergarten in Watertown, Wisconsin, in 1856. And even if it was not the very first kindergarten in the United States, there is no doubt about her influence in having Froebel's methods for rearing small children accepted in America.

One can safely assume that through the first third of the 19th century, the German immigrants influenced primarily America's religious life and the folk-culture of the "common" people. They were also active in some fields of science, in the distribution of books and the founding of newspapers. In the period from the beginning of the American Revolution to the consolidation of the new nation, the war with England of 1812 and the Napoleonic Wars in Europe ending in 1815 (a period of about forty years), transatlantic contacts between the Old and the New Worlds were either completely severed or badly hampered. This was especially the case with intellectual ties.

But after this long period of interruptions, the intellectual flow in the form of literature, scientific knowledge and the fine arts from Germany (and other parts of Europe) to the United States soon swelled again and became wider and deeper than ever before. Among those responsible for this were the English author Thomas Carlyle and the Franco-Swiss author Madame Germaine de Staël, whose book "De l'Allemagne" (on Germany) increased American interest in German intellectual life when it appeared in an English translation in New York in 1814. This marks the beginning of a period in which fiction by German classic, idealistic and romantic authors found an audience in the United States. This was also the case with the great philosophers,

Immanuel Kant and Friedrich Hegel, and the significant political economist Friedrich List. He settled in America and became the father of American trade protectionism. List proposed the introduction of high customs tariffs and titled this policy the "American System" and a "Declaration of Economic Independence". His idea was to make America's economy competitive with that of Great Britain.

In 1827, Francis Lieber settled in America as correspondent for several German newspapers. In his spare time he worked together with many important Americans on the "Encyclopedia Americana" (later "Appleton's American Encyclopedia") with its strong emphasis on German civilization, thereby injecting elements of German spirit into the minds of its readers. Through the many books he authored, Lieber also exerted considerable influence on American political philosophy; he corrected the science of natural right and, based on Kant and rational judgement, promoted the idea of adherence to order as decreed by lawful government.

America was aware of the "Storm and Stress" phase in German literature (as expressed in Goethe's "The Suffering of Young Werther" or in Friedrich Schiller's drama "The Robbers"). But German literature really only became popular in America after 1815. Goethe, Schiller, Körner, Geibel, Rückert, Uhland, Freiligrath, Heinrich Heine, Bürger, Klopstock, the Schlegel brothers, Jean Paul, Herder or Lessing— there is hardly a German literary name whose works were not translated and which were not mentioned in American magazines and literary reviews.

Even third-rate German authors were able to capture the fancy of American readers: one need only to mention forgotten writer Berthold Auerbach and his novels on peasant life, such as his "Black Forest Tales", filled with rural scenes. Between 1864 and 1879, there were twenty American editions of twelve works by Auerbach alone. Even many other obscure authors, predominantly women of the so-called "Gartenlaube school" of fiction, had tremendous success in America. No less than 27 historical novels by Klara Mundt (who wrote under the pseudonym "Luise Mühlbach") were distributed throughout America between 1860 and World War I. Many of these works were romantic exaltations of the simple life, a trend which still can be found today in much of American art.

But, on the other hand, America hardly took notice of the works of Germany's social critics of the late 19th century and such authors as Gerhard Hauptmann and Hermann Sudermann as well as the philosophers Friedrich Nietzsche and Arthur Schopenhauer. In the beginning of the 20th century, with the coming of industrialization to the Western World, the gerat epoch of expressive intellectualism (in which so much of what the German people contributed to the world had been transposed to America) began to fade away. Now, purely scientific knowledge which can be applied to technology gained in importance.

But German participation also in this field of creativity in America remained considerable, despite interruptions caused by the two World Wars. The emigration of Jewish and other prosecuted Germans during the Nazi period, including a dozen Nobel prize winners, among them physicist and mathematician Albert Einstein, greatly enriched America's intellectual life. He and his specialist colleague Hans Bethe were among the famous European scientists who helped America along the road toward becoming an atomic power.

Robert Oppenheimer, the "father of the atomic bomb", and numerous other American scientists had studied in Göttingen when this German university enjoyed a short golden period in the field of nuclear physics. When it became known shortly before the second World War broke out that German chemist Otto Hahn and his co-worker Fritz Strassmann had discovered nuclear fission, when rumors began to circulate that the Germans were in a position to use atomic energy for military purposes, physicist Leo Szilard (a Hungarian-born student of German professors who had emigrated to the United States) convinced Albert Einstein to take an unusual step: in 1939, he prompted the world famous scientist to write a letter of warning to President Franklin D. Roosevelt. In 1940, Einstein repeated his warning that the Germans might be able to develop atomic weapons. As it turned out, the Germans did not, thanks to Hitler's ignorance and his failure to properly evaluate the potential of atomic power. But Roosevelt did, indeed, comprehend its significance. And thus, following appeals from Einstein and other scientists, the "Manhattan Project" was born and it led the United States to become the first atomic power in the world.

The application of nuclear energy for military purposes (which today determines the balance of power between the United States and the Soviet Union) first achieved its full deployment in connection with missiles. And again Germans after 1945 made the decisive contribution to America. By that time, of course, they were not prompted by Nazi terror to emigrate, nor did they decide to leave their country completely on their own. They were talked into doing so by American specialists who (in the course of "Operation Paperclip") set out to round up German scientists to work for America. They succeeded in recruiting most of the German rocket specialists who had developed the "retaliation weapons" V-1 and V-2 in Peenemünde during the war. After all, these were weapons which had reached London from the European Continent.

The most famous of the immigrant German rocket specialists is

Wernher von Braun who, by developing the Saturn rocket, made possible the first manned space flight to the moon. But he is not alone. Working with him in America were more than two hundred German space flight experts. They came in two groups to the United States, which, for its part, provided them with an opportunity to continue and intensify their pioneering. Among them are experts in all of the complicated and specialized fields: Ernst Stuhlinger for general research, Hermann Weidner for rocket propulsion, Walter Häussermann for steering systems, Willy Mrazek for spaceship construction and mechanics, Ernst Debus for test flights. Debus eventually became Director of the Cape Canaveral Space Center in Florida, from where the Apollo teams took off for the moon.

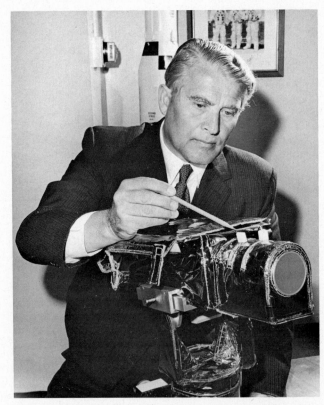

German rocket expert Wernher von Braun lifted American astronauts on the moon

Many other names could be mentioned, including that of Professor Kurzweg of the University of Maryland. In a thousand-foot testing chute in Silver Spring, Maryland, he carries out tests necessary for the construction of ballistic missiles such as the "Polaris". And there is Professor Rudolf Hermann, co-developer of the spacelab.

As Director of the George C. Marshall Space Flight Center and the person responsible for the development of large rockets for NASA, Wernher von Braun has been able to help America overcome the shock it felt on October 4, 1957, when a Soviet "Sputnik" became the first satellite to circle the earth. The Russian radio signals from outer space which caused the "Sputnik-shock" announced to the world that America's great antagonist had been able to take the lead in building rockets. The military significance of this event—the fact that America was now vulnerable to Soviet nuclear missiles—encouraged the Kremlin leadership, at that time headed by ebullient and seemingly incalculable Premier Nikita Khrushchev to speak in bolder and more aggressive terms in world politics.

But soon America had reconquered its world leadership in space exploration and in the construction of military missiles. When astronaut Neil A. Armstrong became the first human being to set foot on the moon (July 20, 1969) and said "That's one small step for man, one giant leap for mankind," he spoke with a background of years of effort and achievement, not least by the German scientists who had emigrated to the United States after 1945. Together with their American colleagues and with the support of America's financial resources and its inexhaustible technical and industrial potential, they had participated in achieving President John F. Kennedy's goal of America reaching the moon before the end of the Sixties. At no time in previous history had such a large, professionally-homogeneous group of Germans played such a prominent role in a project so vital to America as these rocket builders led by Wernher von Braun.

But let us turn back once more from the present to Germans of the past who were able to make a place for themselves in the history of the United States. One of the most prominent of them is the journalist John Peter Zenger. In his "New York Weekly Journal", Zenger waged a crusade against corrupt practices of the British colonial administration and because of it was brought to trial in 1735. English law at that time decreed that a printed attack on a public official (whether true or false) was libelous. Zenger was defended by Philadelphia attorney Andrew Hamilton, a masterful tactician. He convinced the jury that his client had a right to attack the British Governor because his accusations were true. The jury of colonists, Hamilton maintained, was vested with the prerogative to decide the issue of law as well as the truthfulness of Zenger's accusations. The defendant was acquitted and Zenger's trial gained historic importance: the decision was a giant step toward freedom of the press, a freedom which today is one of America's most treasured constitutional rights.

German immigrant Jacob Leisler from Frankfurt on the Main fared a much worse fate. He had settled in New York as a successful trader and shipowner and was appointed Lieutenant Governor and Commander in Chief of the colony by the Dutch colonialists in their 1689 rebellion against King James II. But a year later, the British regained control of the rebellious colony. On May 19, 1691, Leisler and his son-in-law were executed for high treason in New York at the site where today the "Tombs" are located. It was not until five years later that his relatives were able to obtain his posthumous rehabilitation through a petition to the British Parliament and the restoration of the family's property and civil rights. Leisler was probably the first outstandig American of German origin who came to the aid of the common people, assuming the role of a democratic leader in the struggle against the rule and privileges of the Tory aristocracy.

The beginning of the American Revolution in 1775 found Germans on both sides; it is estimated that four-fifths of them were on the side of the revolutionaries and only one-fifth sided with the British. The German settlers took up arms and joined their new countrymen in their battle for independence as soon as the break with England became final. There were some German officers among the foreigners on George Washington's staff who volunteered their talents as professional soldiers to help the Americans to victory.

On the other side, the British employed many regiments of Hessian mercenaries who were herded together by their masters like slaves and sold to the English. And these marcenaries, sent into battle with little pay and even less personal engagement, began to plunder and soon reaped the hatred of their opponents. Since the conflict was not really their concern, many German mercenaries deserted and settled in the German villages and cities in Pennsylvania, Maryland and New Jersey. It is estimated that the British paid the rulers of six German principalities about seven million pounds sterling for thirty thousand Hessian mercenaries. Of these, 12,500 did not return home and it is assumed that only half of them died on the battlefield. The remaining six thousand probably deserted and preferred to begin a new life among the colonists whom they were supposed to fight.

One American settler of German origin who made a name for himself in the Revolutionary War was Nicholas Herkimer, a prosperous businessman living in the Mohawk Valley in the State of New York. When the fighting broke out, he organized four batallions made up primarily of Germans and waged war in the guerilla style of the Indians. In the summer of 1777, these small forces confronted the British marching from Canada to Fort Schuyler. This was the Battle of Oriskany, in which the Americans suffered heavy losses. But Herkimer's forces were able to win valuable time and this (in combination with military successes several months later) brought about one of the turning points in the war: the surrender of British General Burgoyne at Saratoga. Herkimer was severely wounded in the Battle of Oriskany and died a few days later after having his leg amputated.

There was a similar heroic episode in the life of Johann Kalb, who came to America with French General Lafayette. Kalb was born the son of a Franconain farmer. After he married a rich Dutch woman, he assumed the title of "Baron". Baron de Kalb offered his services to George Washington. He was given the rank of Major-General and proved to be an experienced, cold-blooded and cautious military strategist as Commander in the New Jersey and Maryland campaigns. In the Battle of Camden in 1780 (in which Lord Cornwallis' experienced and well-equipped troops forced the untested American militia regiments under the command of General Horatio Gates to retreat), the division of men from Maryland and Delaware led by Baron Johann de Kalb held their position and even managed to launch counterattacks. But in this battle, Kalb, a huge man, was wounded eleven times by musket fire and bayonet thrusts and had to be carried off the field by his soldiers. He succumbed to his wounds three days later.

Other known German officers in the American Revolutionary Forces were Baron von Weissenfels and Major Emanuel Lutterloh, who was appointed Quartermaster General of the Continental Army in 1780. But of the many Germans who are known to have played a role in the War of Independence, only one name has really been remembered: Friedrich Wilhelm von Steuben. Von Steuben served in Frederick the Great's army (where he rose to the rank of Captain) until the end of the Seven Year War. He was discharged by the king because he participated in a duel. But before he left His Majesty's Service, the king promoted him to the rank of Major. Nevertheless, he returned to civilian life almost penniless. After serving several south German courts as chamberlain, he managed to get to America via France in 1777. He immediately wrote George Washington a flamboyant letter offering his experience and talents: "The object of my greatest ambition is to render your country all the services in my power and to deserve the title of a Citizen of America by fighting for the cause of liberty."

Von Steuben apparently had a feeling for the mentality of Americans, and for their weak spots. In any case, he introduced himself to George Washington as "Lieutenant-General" and "Baron" to make himself as attractive as possible. And Washington could not afford to be choosy. He was just preparing for the tough winter at Valley Forge and probably was delighted that in this desperate situation what appeared to be such an outstanding commander of foreign armies would offer him his services.

Regardless of how braggartly Steuben had behaved at the beginning, his experiences as a former officer under Frederich II turned out to be invaluable to the most inexperienced Continental Army forces, which at this time had shrunk to barely five thousand men. Washington appointed Steuben "Inspector General with overall responsibility for military discipline, instruction and supply". And indeed, Steuben went about training and drilling the soldiers with great skill; he also wrote the first manual of army regulations.

Despite a lack of even bare essentials, Steuben drilled his men from morning to night, firing them on with his spicy language and his own ebullience. And in the winter of 1777—1778, the untiring Prussian officer (who could not even speak English) was actually able to assemble a half-way powerful striking force. Next to the Frenchman Marquis de Lafayette, General Baron von Steuben was the most successful foreign officer in training and assembling the first American regular forces, the Continental Army under the Supreme Command of General George Washington.

This Prussian drillmaster taught his men to exercise and to attack in orderly formation according to Prussian tactics but adapted to fit American conditions. In contrast to other European officers, Steuben maintained close contact with the simple soldier and demonstrated understanding for the democratic attitude taken by his subordinates. In a letter to a friend in Germany he wrote: "The genius of this nation is not to be compared with that of the Prussians, Austrians or French. You say to your soldier, 'do this', and he doeth it; but I am obliged to say, 'this is the reason why you ought to do that', and then he doeth it."

It is not known whether Washington ever found out that the man he appointed to be his Inspector General in reality had been nothing more than a discharged Captain. But apparently the American Supreme Commander was only interested in Steuben's performance and achievements, and they were impressive. In any case, Friedrich Wilhelm von Steuben was promoted to the rank of Major-General (this time for real) and the appointment was confirmed by the Continental Congress. After the war, Steuben retired with a yearly pension of 2,500 dollars and owned sixteen thousand acres of land which the State of New York gave him. And if Steuben was somewhat of a soldier of fortune, there is no doubt that he was successful; his employers, indeed, got what they paid for.

Major General Friedrich Wilhelm von Steuben trained George Washington's men at Valley Forge

When British Commander Lord Cornwallis capitulated to the American Forces on October 19, 1781 in Yorktown, Virginia, Steuben was among the Generals placed behind George Washington. The painting which depicts this historic event immortalizes German participation in America's struggle for independence. Friedrich Wilhelm von Steuben became the national hero of generations of German-Americans and is commemorated every year in a series of "Steuben-Parades", the most famous of which are in New York and Chicago. This is one of the very few German—American folkloristic events which resound beyond the confines of the immediate area where they are held and which recall a small but significant remnant of German—American ties.

In the past several decades, the name Steuben is mentioned in the same breath with that of Carl Schurz, even though their presence in America was three fourths of a century apart and they had little in common in their origins, professions, political goals or activities. The memory of these two men has been kept alive since 1948 by the "Steuben—Schurz Society", the successor to the "Steuben Society", which was founded in 1919. But the only thing the two men really had in common was that they were able to gain outstanding positions in American public life. And it should be mentioned that Carl Schurz's intellectual and political achievements have left behind a much more significant legacy than Steuben's military heritage.

Carl Schurz, the most important German—American, lived in Germany during a period of awakening and upheaval. That was the epoch in which the Germans—later in history than any other European people —began to declare themselves in favor of a national unitary state under a democratic system of government. Schurz was born near the Rhine city of Cologne in 1829. He was barely twenty when he was caught up as a student in the turbulence of revolts and demonstrations which for the first time shook the absolute rule of the German sovereigns. As a man of action, he participated in the revolt against the reign of the Prussians in the Rhineland and in the Palatinate and was forced to flee when the rebellion was crushed. After having organized a spectacular escape of his friend and teacher Professor Gottfried Kinkel from a prison in Spandau (near Berlin)—which gained Schurz both admiration and notoriety all over Europe—, he managed to reach New York with his young wife in 1852. It was only a few years later that this young, liberal revolutionary was to play an important role in the political life of his new homeland.

In contrast to some "Forty-Eighters" who had fled to America from the German states to avoid political persecution, Schurz had no inclinations whatsoever toward creating autonomous organizations or founding a German state within the United States. He became an American citizen in 1857, and (with the financial support of his wife's Jewish family in Hamburg) was able to survive as a journalist, orator and lecturer in Wisconsin. Soon his mastery of the English language was such that one could hardly tell him apart from a native American.

At first, Schurz believed that America could be moved to intervene in Europe on the side of the democratic—liberal freedom movements. In 1852 he wrote, "America could become the fatherland of Europe's freedom. Democracy has a certain standing as soon as America participates." But it was not long before he abandoned this hope and, encouraged by businessmen of German origin in Wisconsin, began to participate actively in American domestic politics.

These were the years in which the differences between the agricultural South and the industrial North became more and more pronounced. With the abolishment of slavery, the conflict eventually erupted into the Civil War, a war which Schurz had predicted would come. He also foresaw that the Union would defeat the Confederacy. As far as Schurz was concerned, slavery was America's "central conflict". But mismanagement caused by the spoils system was the other dark spot in his view of the United States.

The progressive wing of the Republican Party provided Carl Schurz with a platform from which he could exert political influence on America. He articulated his thoughts on "true Americanism" in a famous speech in Boston's Faneuil Hall. With brilliant eloquence, he stated his belief that America had a special responsibility and obligation to lead humanity toward Democracy, and his speech alluded strongly to America's Messianic calling, toward which Presidents Woodrow Wilson and Franklin Roosevelt were later to gear their foreign policies.

Carl Schurz the orator was a combination of German idealism and American pragmatism. Schurz's speeches unfolded a treasury of liberal thoughts which enriched American thinking with broad-mindedness and humaneness and gained him access to the company of such luminaries as Ralph Waldo Emerson, Oliver Wendell Holmes and Henry Wadsworth Longfellow. At the historic Republican Party Convention in Chicago's "Wigwam", Schurz and the delegation from Wisconsin gave their votes on the third ballot to Abraham Lincoln, who therewith got the party's nomination for the presidency. And Carl Schurz had the honor of heading the delegation which brought the news of "Abe's" nomination to Lincoln in Springfield, Illinois. Lincoln went after the German—American vote quite early in his political career. And many states were carried for Lincoln by the German—American vote.

Schurz did not have to wait very long for his reward for this, perhaps, decisive aid during the presidential campaign. Immediately after his inauguration, Lincoln appointed Schurz American envoy to Spain. But in Madrid, he was not at all captivated by his duties, which were primarily focused on maintaining Spain's neutrality in the American Civil War. Schurz recognized the conflict between the Union and the Confederacy as the decisive development in consolidating America as a nation and he could not stand his inactivity in Madrid any longer.

Carl Schurz's activities as American Minister at the Court of Queen Isabella lasted for less than a year. He asked President Lincoln to relieve him of his diplomatic duties so that he could join the Union forces as a soldier to fight the Civil War. In 1862, he returned to the United States. At the age of thirty-three, Schurz was made brigadier general, a purely political appointment since the young officer had had very little practical experience as a soldier. His military knowledge was limited mainly to reading books by Clausewitz, Frederick the Great and Napoleon I. But appointments of that kind were not at all unusual for those times.

Schurz's participation in some of the great battles as division commander did not earn him any particular distinction. His troops were involved in the unfortunate retreat after the second Battle of Bull Run and the catastrophic defeat of the Union Forces at Chancellorsville. But Schurz and his men were also present at the decisive victory of the Union at Gettysburg. Thus, he fought the Civil War with more enthusiasm than success. But for Schurz, the political meaning of this bloody struggle was fulfilled when (following the Battle of Antietam) President Lincoln published the preliminary proclamation on the abolition of slavery.

In these years, a close but somewhat one-sided relationship had developed between the President and Schurz. He and his wife were frequent guests at the White House and the German-American hardly missed an oppurtunity to bombard the Chief Executive with letters of warning or advice. Lincoln sometimes was encouraged by what Schurz wrote him, but from time to time he gently but firmly rebuked his German-American friend. In one answer, Lincoln admonished Schurz in the following terms: "Be assured, my dear Sir, there are men that think you are performing your part as poorly as you think I am performing mine." But the great admiration which these two men had for each other remained unaffected, and Schurz took the President's assassination as a deep personal loss.

But the death of Abraham Lincoln did not mark the end of either Carl Schurz's literary or political career. In 1869, he was elected U.S. Senator from Missouri. During his six years in the Senate, Schurz fought in Congress for the reform of the civil service with the goal of replacing the spoils and patronage system with an appointment system based on merit, somewhat along German lines. But at that time America had not yet matured to the point of accepting such changes. His chance to push for this reform from another vantage point came in 1877, when President Rutherford B. Hayes appointed Schurz Secretary of the Interior. And becoming a cabinet member was the high point of the public career of the now 48-year old immigrant; the first American of German descent to be given a cabinet post.

As Secretary of the Interior, Schurz continued his campaign for creating a more modern bureaucracy, but without much success. He also stubbornly fought for an improvement of the lot of the American Indian, most of whom had been driven from their homes and into reservations. He uprooted parasitic officeholders in the Bureau of Indian Affairs, created some schools for the Red Man and favored allotment of land to the Indians. In these endeavors he was opposed by the U.S. Army, and he again fought without much success. "Here was a man who wanted to see absolute justice done to the Indian, to the Negro and to the southern White Man," a prominent American later said about Schurz and his efforts. And as Secretary of the Interior, which he remained for four years (through 1881), Schurz also established himself as a forerunner of today's environmentalists. He fought for the conservation of the American forests and tried—again with very little success— to reduce the ruthless exploitations of forests by commercial interests.

Carl Schurz was not at all free of vanity, egocentricity or dogmatism. But these human weaknesses were completely overshadowed by his idealism and his sense of justice as liberal humanist. Gradually he identified himself entirely with his new homeland and once summed up his belief in America with the words, "Genuine Americanism will emerge from the best thoughts of Europe, but beyond that will bring additional progress. The genuine American must be a creative World Citizen."

Schurz had an astonishing talent for analytical foresight. In 1855, one-hundred years before West Germany's entry into NATO, he observed, "Germany is the only power in Europe whose interests will not conflict with those of America, and America is the only power in the civilized world which need not be jealous of a strong, united Germany."

And the accuracy of this statement was not affected in its essence by the great military conflicts between the United States and Germany in the two World Wars. These confrontations did not originate from fundamental American-German rivalries but were a consequence of European tragedies.

Beyond the successes of his political career, Schurz as an individual was a classic example of the quick transformation of the immigrant into the American citizen. And thereby he was a complete adversary of the short-lived movement aimed at gaining for Germany autonomy within the United States, which began after 1830. What gave rise to this movement were the anti-foreigner attitude of the Anglo-Americans (directed especially against the Irish and the Germans) and the tendencies of the German settler groups to try to maintain their German cultural heritage and protect it from foreign influences. These "protectors of Germanity" and their organizations (such as the Giessen Society, an offshoot of the type of dueling university fraternity peculiar to Germany) believed that if they couldn't establish democracy in Germany, then they could do so completely unmolested in America. But, they believed, this should definitely not include the absorption of the German immigrant into Anglo-American culture. As far as they were concerned, it would have been ideal to simply establish a "New Germany" in America. And American soil appeared to them to be very fertile for this in some parts of Wisconsin, Illinois, Ohio, Michigan and Minnesota, where large numbers of Germans had settled.

These tendencies were viewed with concern by some American politicians, not least because several fiery and almost fanatical advocates of a "New Germany" (such as Dr. Ludwig Brauns) actually went on crusades to preserve the German language in America and against the "melting" of German immigrants with other ethnic groups. One other crusader was Franz Lohrer. He went so far as to say that the Germans "can have German schools and universities, German literature and art, German science and philosophy, German courts and assemblies—in short, they can have a German state in which the German language is as much the popular and official language as English is now, and in which the German spirit rules."

However, more moderate German—Americans immediately recognized the dangers of these separatist tendencies; that behavior such as that recommended by the founder of the Giessen Society, Paul Follen, could only reap the antagonism of their fellow citizens. Follen wanted "the foundation of a new and free Germany in the great North American Republic." The members of the "New German Society of Philadelphia" had similar ideas: in 1836 they suggested that in partial isolation they would be able to enjoy both the advantages of America and the pleasures of the fatherland.

These efforts climaxed for several years in the German conventions organized from 1837 with the purpose of convincing the German settlers to establish a German Commonwealth and preserving German culture in America. But fortunately again there were moderate German—Americans (like Gustav Koerner and Francis Lieber) who came to grips with this enthusiasm and were able to cool it off before it did any damage. Thus, German separatism on American soil never amounted to much more than a tragicomedy and never became a serious issue. The sporadic conflicts between German autonomists and American nativists hostile to foreigners, such as the followers of the "Know-nothing Movement", did not raise any serious doubts in the minds of most Americans as to the desirability of assimilation. In fact, the industrialization of America, which was in full swing by this time, only increased their willingness to "melt".

Other "Forty-Eighters" besides Carl Schurz became well known:

Franz Sigel, Friedrich Hecker and August Willich. The number of political refugees who emigrated to America following the dissolution of the German National Assembly in Frankfurt in 1849 was approximately two thousand. Several hundred of them eventually returned to Germany. Many thought that they would only have to seek temporary refuge in America because conditions in Germany would soon improve or America would intervene in Europe on the side of the democratic forces. Both expectations turned out to be unfounded. But before this became evident, some auf these intellectual "Forty-Eighters" (among them freethinkers, atheists and radical social reformers) managed to upset a number of conservative, staid Americans. It took a while for these immigrants to overcome their illusions and to permit themselves to be absorbed and incorporated into the American mainstream.

The masses of immigrants which arrived in America during the middle of the century brought many Germans who had no other choice but to begin their new lives in the slums of the large cities. Tension erupted between the German settlers who had established themselves financially and socially and the newcomers. This was similar to the friction which developed between other ethnic groups of the "lower" classes. But the approaching American Civil War overshadowed this dissonance. And when the Germans for the first time voted overwhelmingly Republican in support of Abraham Lincoln, they did so less with an eye on the abolition of slavery or other issues between the Confederacy and the Union. They were motivated much more to vote for the Republican candidate because Lincoln had promised to oppose laws which had been passed in some states under pressure from American nativists and Know-nothing supporters. These laws limited the civil rights of newly-arrived immigrants, including their right to vote and to hold public office. And his election, indeed, prevented the spreading of such restrictive laws which would have created a deep rift between the established Americans and the newcomers, including the many Germans.

In the Civil War, the Germans—just like all Americans—could be found fighting on both sides. In the Union Army their numbers were proportionately much higher than their numerical presence in the population. Proportionately there were more Germans in the Union Army than either native Americans or Irish immigrants. Historians today are not agreed on the military achievements of the Germans during the Civil War. The fact that the XI. Corps of the Army of the Potomac (made up mostly of Germans) was overrun by Confederate General Thomas "Stonewall" Jackson's troops in the Battle of Chancellorsville and that the divisions of General Schurz and Steinwehr were forced to retreat had given the German units the nickname the "Flying Dutchmen". But historians agree that some of the responsibility for these military failures can be attributed to the American commanders of troops at Chancellorsville, such as Major General Joe Hooker and the Commander of the XI. Corps, General O. Howard, who had failed to give their German subordinates enough warning of enemy troop movements.

In the later stages of the war, the German—American soldiers of the Union Army were able to rehabilitate their reputation at Gettysburg, in the storming of Lookout Mountain and General Sherman's attack on Atlanta. They are said to have fought those battles with outstanding courage. In the Union Army, "Forty-Eighters" Schurz, Sigel and Willich and other Americans of German origin held the rank of general. History records that on the other side there also were officers of German descent fighting enthusiastically for the Confederacy, including brigadier general Louis A. Armistead, a descendant of the German family Armstadt, brigadier general James L. Kemper and others. One name deserves to be mentioned for an entirely different reason: German Count Zeppelin, who served in the Union Army as an engineer, gained some experience in military aviation with observation balloons and then returned to Germany to build the famous dirigibles named after him.

Wherever in the two World Wars German-Americans fought Germans, they frequently performed with special diligence and courage and their stories often became legends. One need only mention the flying aces of the first world war, Captain Eddie Rickenbacker (Richenbacher) and Lieutenant Frank Luke, or a young officer who served in World War II, Lieutenant Karl H. Timmermann. He secured the bridge over the Rhine River at Remagen so that the advancing troops could continue their march into the heartland of Germany.

Wherever the German immigrants settled down—the farmers and sectarians of the 17th and 18th centuries, the industrial workers and intellectuals of the 19th century and the scientists, technicians and businessmen of our time—, wherever they found a political home in America they demonstrated an especially strong interest in influencing the platforms or ideologies of both the Republicans and Democrats. Indeed, there were times—above all in the middle of the 19th century—when they tried to bring their weight to bear by voting as a block. But by and large in the American two-party system, they did not attempt to act as a clearly distinguishable ethnic grouping with special political interests. The only inclination in that direction could be found (and then only temporarily) among the "Forty-Eighters", some of whom were ultra-liberal and some the pupils of Karl Marx, with distinct socialist ideas.

An interesting if short episode concerning the activities of the original leftist German-Americans was their participation in the formation of socialist parties in the United States. One of the most active members of the American section of the First International was "Forty-Eighter" F. A. Sorge. German workers made up most of the membership of the Socialist Labor Party founded in 1877. This was also the case with the more moderate Social Democratic Party, which was established a few years later.

The Social Democratic Party became the Socialist Party in 1901 and was led by Eugene V. Debs, whose parents had come from Alsace. He received about 900,000 votes (or six per cent) in his third try for the presidency in 1912. And that has remained the most significant success of politically-organized socialism in America even to this day. Debs got many votes from Americans of German descent, especially in Milwaukee, Wisconsin.

The Jews who came to America from Germany to seek freedom were a special category of persecuted persons. They were mostly families which had once been integrated into the German states, Jew from the German-language areas of the Austrian-Hungarian Monarchy and from the east European Yiddish-speaking areas. Consequently, not every American Jew with a German-sounding name was originally a German Jew. But they all had one thing in common: until late in the 19th century, they had all been the victims of legal, social and religious discrimination, of being kept confined to ghettos and of being periodically persecuted for various and sundry reasons. They had more reason than any other ethnic or religious grouping to leave central and eastern Europe. This pressure first subsided with the liberalization of central Europe, which brought a strong influx of east European Jews to Germany and to the states of the Austrian Monarchy.

But what in the middle of the 19th century had become a refuge for these fleeing Jews (and had brought Germany tremendous assets in the form of achievement, intelligence, acumen and artistic creativity) became hell on earth with the beginning of National Socialist rule. The Jews in Germany immediately became the object of persecution and eventually the victims of systematic, barbaric genocide. Nothing in all of history burdened German—American relations as heavily as Hitler's racist insanity and its horrible and unforgettable consequences: the "final solution" gas chambers of Auschwitz and other death camps as well as the mass-executions carried out in eastern Europe by Heinrich Himmler's special commandoes of killers known as the "SS", the black-uniformed men sworn to protect Adolf Hitler.

During and even after this organized butchery and official brutality, it must have been shocking and unacceptable for many Jews who had at one time emigrated from Germany to America to be considered a "German" immigrant. But it was precisely those Jews who had fled Germany who so greatly enriched America in the fields of finance, trade, science and art and who were outstanding in social work and philanthropy.

One need only mention the names of a few of the many Jewish families which achieved prosperity and esteem and which today exert considerable influence in America to illustrate how foolish and disastrous this exodus war for Germany. There are the Guggenheims, one of the wealthiest families in the United States; their forefathers emigrated to America from a small village near Heidelberg, where they had come from Switzerland. The Rothschilds came from Frankfurt and other European cities; the Warburgs had been bankers in Germany; the Seligmans were originally from Bavaria; the Belmonts were still known as the Schönbergs when they left the Rhineland Palatinate and Lehman, Schiff, Speyer, Loeb, Kahn, Morgenthau, Hallgarten, Goldman or Wertheim; this is but a small collection of Jewish names traceable to Germany which today are respected and exert influence far beyond the borders of the United States. When these families first came to America they formed such a close, almost aristocratic community, that they dubbed themselves the "One Hundred". And with a claim to exclusivity in prosperity, education and good breeding, they differentiated between themselves and the poorer Jewish immigrants from Europe who soon referred to them as the "Jewish Grand Dukes".

But it was an "outsider" of German—Jewish origin whose name pushed all of the others into the shadows of the "international spotlight": Henry A. Kissinger, Secretary of State and National Security Advisor to two American Presidents. Under the pressure of Nazi rule, the Kissinger family had been forced to leave the town of Fürth in Bavaria and to emigrate to America.

Many individuals stand out from the manifold and shapeless mass of German—Americans from all walks of life. The Germans, however, were only co-architects of American civilization; they did not shape it alone. The lack of significant American politicians of German descent —with only a few exceptions—underlines this. The bulk of German influence on the United States was brought to bear by the millions of farmers, farm hands, craftsmen, tradesmen, educators and skilled as well as unskilled workers who came to America as nameless immigrants. They were good leavened dough for America and they contributed much to the capabilities of the United States. In some professions Germans became known as the experts. For instance in beer brewing. And that is why Milwaukee (once known as "German Athens" because of its many theaters, operas and glee clubs) the home of such famous brands as Schlitz, Pabst and Miller, became known as "The German Beer-Capital of the U.S.A."

"Kraut", the American nickname for Germans, stems from the cliché-impressions many Americans have of the "typical German": sturdy, robust, easy-going and somewhat awkward. And this nickname has stuck to the Germans as much as the name "Limey" follows the Englishmen and Frenchmen are known in the U.S. as "Frogs". These terms often reflect quite aptly (but are not always applicable at all times to all persons) the feeling of one people for some of the traits of another people. The image which the Germans have had in America has varied considerably as the result of the variations in German—American relations and the differences between the types of immigrant-groups.

But despite the changing times and conditions, the two peoples have some hard set notions about each other which have not changed. The American therefore still tends to think of Germany in terms of sauerkraut and Heidelberg, marching and subservient housewives concerned only with their kitchen, children and church, even though these characteristics are no longer really typical of today's Germany. And in cases when these shades of clichés ranging from primitive joy of life and homey romanticism to discipline, arrogance and subservience are benevolently enriched, then the educated German in America is relegated to academic society (even if he does not belong there at all) and is often addressed as "Doctor" regardless of whether he has any claim to the title.

The American, for his part, still is viewed in Germany according to a fixed pattern. Especially in earlier times he was the "rich uncle" who just had to be eccentric. The impression of American women (taken from Hollywood) has been that they all have been divorced at least four times. And if the Germans think of America in terms of big cities or wide open spaces, then they are bound to think of Americans as gangsters, cowboys and sheriffs, or at least as the uncultured, tough businessman who drives around in his big car weaving through skyscrapers. But all in all, the German in general views the American more positively (with a teaspoon of respect and a tablespoon of admiration) than the average American views the German.

Since few Americans settle down in Germany but millions of Germans have made new homes in America, the transfusion of customs and ways of life was somewhat one-sided until the age of mass communication. This is particularly evident in the take-over of foreign words in language. In America, typical terms from the German languages are in common usage in only three or four specific fields: food, the military, politics and philosophy. Americans eat *hamburgers* and *frankfurters, sauerbraten* and *sauerkraut* and wash them down with a stein of beer. They are as familiar with a *panzer* as with the *blitzkrieg.* If some public figure comes under fire, he gets a lot of *flak* (taken from the German abbreviation of anti-aircraft artillery). There is no appropriate substitute in English for *Ostpolitik* or *Realpolitik.* And the German's intermittent craving for *lebensraum* can, as was clearly demonstrated, lead them into *goetterdaemmerung.*

Vice versa with the outbreak of the era oriented toward technology and communication, innumerable Americanisms have taken a permanent place in the German vernacular, especially in slang or when the subjects are sports, business and military technology. Every German understands *O. K.* as well as he does *K. O.* If he gets too fat, he takes it off with *fitness-training.* As a businessman he is concerned with *management* and *computers.* And than he wonders, perhaps, whether the United States is tending more toward a *first strike strategy* or will stick to *counterforce.* When he takes leave of his friends he often says *bye-bye.* Somewhere in the background a *band* is playing and the German *teenagers* in their *blue jeans* are dancing *rock 'n roll.*

4
Cooperation and conflicts

The War of Independence against the English and its success made it necessary for the United States to establish relations with other nations and to make a place for itself in world politics. Indeed, in his farewell speech to the young nation in 1796, George Washington had cautioned his fellow countrymen: "The great rule of conduct for us in regard to foreign nations is, in extending our commercial relations, to have with them as little political connection as possible ..."

However, even in its initial stages the young nation could not adopt such self-imposed isolationism as an iron-clad guideline. After all, the rebellious colonies were themselves in the midst of a struggle against one European power (Great Britain) with the active support of another European power, France, which, for its part, was allied with Spain against the British. Hence, John Adams, one of the most significant leaders of the revolution, recommended already in the early stages of the struggle: "We ought to send envoys to all great European courts, especially those which are seafaring powers, and have our emissaries propose that they formally recognize America's independence and conclude friendship and trade treaties with the United States. This would be completely in line with America's basic system and would demonstrate the esteem which young nations owe to older ones."

This was put into practice, and soon emissaries swarmed out from the Continental Congress to the European courts. The most outstanding of these were Benjamin Franklin, Thomas Jefferson, Arthur Lee, Silas Deane and John Adams. They skillfully made use of European intrigues and entanglements and exploited them for their own purposes. The first major success of this initial American diplomatic offensive on the Old Continent came in 1783, with the Peace of Paris, in which the English King acknowledged the United States "... to be free, sovereign and independent states." Thus, the Americans had been able to reach their primary goal without even entering into any specific obligations or ties themselves.

The newly-created state entered into its first official relations in 1778, when it concluded a friendship, trade and alliance treaty with France. This was soon followed by trade agreements with Holland (1782) and

Sweden (1783). As a matter of fact, in the course of the War of Independence, first contacts had been established with Prussia, which was then the most powerful of the German states. But these contacts at first remained fruitless. Frederick II had good reasons for hesitating: during the Seven Years War, the small "world war" of that epoch (1756—1763), he was an ally of Great Britain and was receiving English subsidies at the very time when the British were trying to take away France's colonies in the New World. They eventually succeeded in getting Canada and all territories east of the Mississippi.

By supporting Prussia, British Prime Minister William Pitt had been able to tie France (which Frederick II was fighting as well as Austria) to a large degree to Europe. Pitt's ingenious idea of gaining the French possessions in America on the battlefields of Germany thereby became reality. It was only after Pitt was dismissed by King George III that relations between Prussia and England cooled noticeably and to the point that British subsidies no longer flowed to Berlin. Frederick II took this change of attitude amiss and began to become friendly toward the American colonies which were fighting England. It was his intention thus to improve the economic condition of his own war-torn country by intensifying its foreign trade.

As early as March, 1776, Silas Deane sent a message from his post in Paris to the U. S. Congress that (after the division of Poland) the Prussian King wanted to develop his country into a naval power and to have his Baltic Sea ports used for transatlantic trade. Therefore, Deane warned, under no circumstances should the American envoys in Europe bypass Prussia. On the other hand, the Americans were anxious to prevent the Prussian Court from sending German troops to help combat the rebellion in the colonies of North America.

As a result of Deane's advice, the Americans took the initiative in establishing contacts with Prussia and in 1777 sent Arthur Lee (and later his brother William Lee) to Berlin. The Prussian Foreign Minister, Baron von Schulenburg, informed Lee: "Your presence here will not be disagreeable to the King provided that you live here as a private person and do not engage in any official functions." In other words, Frederick II did not want to avoid America as an opponent of Great Britain but (since he could not yet foresee which course the War of Independence would take) did not want to get too close either. The Prussian King simply did not want to risk complications with London.

Consequently, when in June, 1777, Lee sent him a letter, Frederick did not answer. When Lee appealed to him to supply the Americans with artillery, weapons and money, the monarch referred him to von Schulenburg. But Lee was not entirely unsuccessful: in December, 1777, he was able to inform Congress that in answer to his request,

Frederick II had refused permission for soldiers, which Great Britain had recruited from Hesse and Hanau and which were to be sent to America, to march through Prussian territory.

William Lee already visualized the emerging relations with Prussia in the context of greater world political developments. Though these developments never came about, the ideas alone demonstrated Lee's conceptual way of thinking. In December, 1777, he reported to Washington that the friendship with the King of Prussia could be of value, keep Russia in check and prevent it from giving any support to Great Britain as long as England was still engaged in war with America. In those days, American diplomats like Lee thought in terms of the classical European diplomacy of international balance of power.

The following year, the eager envoy pleaded with Frederick II to recognize the United States of America now that France had done so.

The Americans had already let the King know that the presence of their corsairs in north German seaports could be utilized for training German sailors in order to build up a Prussian navy. At that time, however, the Prussians confined themselves to assuring all liberties for American merchants and their ships in Prussian ports. For the Prussian ruler, North America (while still struggling for its independence) apparently was an indefineable entity and, in any case, for the time being of minor importance compared to European nations. These initial Prussian-American contacts were therefore still marking time; Frederick II did not yet want to enter into any firm engagement with the struggling country.

It was not until the Peace of Paris had secured the independence and autonomy of the United States that Frederick was willing to develop relations beyond the stage of initial contacts. On February 18, 1784, the Prussian Envoy to The Hague, Baron Friedrich Wilhelm von Thulemeier, proposed to his American colleague in London, John Adams, that the two countries negotiate a trade agreement modeled after the American-Swedish accord. The negotiations were concluded one year later; a rather quick procedure considering the cumbersome and time-consuming method of conducting diplomatic correspondence in those times.

The first agreement of a German state with the newborn United States bears the signatures of Benjamin Franklin, Thomas Jefferson, John Adams and Baron von Thulemeier. It is dated the 9th and 28th of July, the 5th of August and September 10th, 1785. These were the dates on which the four diplomats signed at four different locations: Jefferson in Paris, Franklin in the Paris suburb of Passy (where he resided), Adams in London and Thulemeier in The Hague. The Ameri-

Frederick the Great, King of Prussia, concluded the first "Treaty of Amity and Commerce" with the USA

can Congress ratified the agreement and it went into effect on May 17, 1786, two months before Frederick the Great died.

This "Treaty of Amity and Commerce" secured for Prussia and the United States a solid, comprehensive and inviolable peace. It gave preference to their mutual trade relations based on the most-favored nation clause and called for reciprocity in the protection of each other's citizens. The agreement provided for the establishment of consulates and, in case of an armed conflict between the two states, for humane treatment of war prisoners. The clauses dealing with the protection of each other's property were exemplary for international law, especially when compared with the way in which these matters

Prince Otto von Bismarck, unifier and Chancellor of the German Reich, advocated non-interference in the Western Hemisphere and a friendly attitude towards the United States

are dealt with today. "This", George Washington wrote approvingly to a friend, "is most liberal agreement ever concluded between two independent powers."

It stands to reason that the generosity contained in this treaty (which went so far as to include guarantees for freedom of religion and acting according to one's own conscience) was not solely because the signatories were obsessed by unlimited idealistic and noble motivations. "The beautiful abstractions" of many of the components of this agreement was made possible rather because there were no points of contention between Prussia and the United States and none were in the offing. The spheres in which their national interests overlapped or confronted each other were minimal. And this was why, with but minor adjustments, this treaty proved to have an unusually long term of life.

Originally the agreement was to be in effect for a period of ten years. It was extended for another ten years and in 1828, following a period in which there was no treaty because of the Napoleonic Wars, it was renegotiated. Beyond its significance as the basis of American-Prussian relations, this treaty served as a model for agreements which the U. S. concluded with other German states.

As German emigration to America continued and the United States began to trade more and more with Germany—first with the Hanseatic coastal cities and then with the rest of the country—, commercial and political ties were such that it became necessary to regulate them on paper. Between 1785 and 1891, the United States concluded no less than 35 conventions and treaties with the individual German states and free trading cities; with Hamburg and Bremen, with Bavaria, Württemberg, Baden and Hannover, with the North German Bund and with the German Reich founded in 1871. These documents were also primarily friendship and trade agreements or conventions covering extradition and naturalization. The latter had become necessary by virtue of the large numbers of Germans who continued to emigrate to America.

The Prussian-American treaty, however, did not bring the boom in trade which it had been intended to promote. Prussia's neutral position during the War of Independence (which permitted France to enter into the American-French alliance so ably promoted in 1778 by Benjamin Franklin) unquestionably brought about a political constellation of the European powers which was of benefit to the United States. And at least in that respect, Prussia played a part in the emergence of the United States as an independent nation. The formal dissolution of the State of Prussia by the allied Four Power Control Council in February of 1947 (in which the United States played no small role) was a sad sequel to what had happened 160 years earlier.

Despite the early diplomatic contacts between America and Prussia, it took until November 11, 1817, before the first German envoy to America, Friedrich von Greuhm, presented his credentials as Minister Resident and Consul-General to President James Monroe in Washington. With but a few exceptions, throughout the 19th century relations between the two countries (just as between the new and the old worlds) concentrated on trade. Diplomatic and political affairs were of secondary importance during that period. And there were objective reasons for this: the "world powers" of that time were the large European states such as Russia, Austria, France, Great Britain and

Germany. One could also include Italy (which was just beginning to emerge as a power) and Spain, which had begun its decline.

In this context, the United States of America played a very modest role. Continental states such as the German Reich (and before that Prussia) did not have the slightest reason to violate the Monroe Doctrine by interfering in the affairs of the Western Hemisphere. And the United States, for its part, had no cause to give up its strict neutrality toward the Europeans, expecially the continental Europeans. The war with Spain was an exception with special reasons. As naval powers of the Atlantic, the United States and Great Britain had common interests to the point of that special relationship which proved so useful in the two World Wars. But in the 19th century, the Atlantic Ocean served as a vacuum in political relations between America and the continental European powers.

Another reason for the lack of political ties to Europe during the infant years of the United States was that at that time both the Europeans and Americans were almost completely absorbed by their internal affairs. In the 19th century, all countries of the Northern Hemisphere developed into industrial states; the United States somewhat more quickly than the countries on the Eastern shores of the Atlantic. In addition, the United States was taken up with the great adventure of pushing the railroad through to America's Pacific coast, and of settling that area of the country.

Though the continental European nations and Great Britain had temporarily put in order their system of balance of power at the Vienna Congress of 1815, it was soon endangered by instability and required repeated renovation. One such renovation was undertaken at the Berlin Congress of 1878, at which Bismarck played the role of the "honest broker", engaging in diplomatic interplay with Disraeli. In the middle of the 19th century, the continental European powers were gripped by rebellious upheavals against feudalistic rule. Countries such as Germany and Italy at that point used the situation to establish their nation-states. And in the cases of divided countries like Poland and in the Austrian-Hungarian Monarchy, a longing for self-determination came to the surface.

On the fringes of its endeavors to achieve German unity through "Blood and Iron", Prussia waged wars against Denmark and Austria and, together with other German states, the 1870—71 war against France. That war brought the annexation of Alsace-Lorraine, which turned out to be one of the important causes of World War I. America and Europe were much too pre-occupied with their own problems to spend much time and energy on intensifying relations across the Atlantic.

This mutualy well-intended lack of interest in each other's affairs, as we shall describe their relations, was again and again played up by them whenever warlike complications threatened to interfere. In fact, Undersecretary of State George Davis, commenting on the German-French war, said in August, 1870, "The United States will stick to its principle of not participating in the political affairs of European powers." In his orders to Germany's Envoy in Washington in December of 1871, Bismarck, for his part, emphasized that the German Reich had absolutely no intention of "wanting to set its foot anywhere in America. We accept without reservation," he continued, "the prevalent influence of the United States on the entire continent as being ingrained in the nature of things and at the same time serving best our own interests. There we have no political, only commercial interests . . ."

A striking example of the secondary role which political relations between the German Reich and the United States played in the Bismarck era can be found in the report which envoy Kurd von Schlözer sent to Berlin in March of 1872. He underlined the fact that during the war with France the German public got excited about English weapons deliveries to the French but hardly took notice of American sales of weapons to Germany's adversary. "If," von Schlözer writes, "we did not take offense at what the one country was doing while being outraged by the same actions of another, it was only because our people instinctively felt that the Yankees were acting merely as businessmen while the British sales of weapons were an act of real animosity toward Germany. The American, in their opinion, was only trying to market his wares where it brought the most profit without any political antipathy or sympathy as a motivation. The United States on the whole is far more distant from us than is generally realized. There are only two European states which have a real political interest in what goes on in North America: England and Spain . . . All other European powers have but a commercial interest in the United States; their political interests are only of secondary importance and can only be affected indirectly by what happens here."

But the fact that until the beginning of the 20th century commercial ties between Europe and the United States were prevalent does not mean that trade relations were exceptionally strong, were entirely without complications or excluded various types of frictions between the two countries. Nevertheless, it should not be forgotten that although the dimensions of foreign trade in those days were almost minimal at the beginning, they were indeed of elementary importance. In the early stages, trade between America and Germany as well as other European nations was confined mainly to agricultural products and raw materials, some of which were almost indispensable to the Europeans. On the other hand, selling its products abroad (such as cotton and tobacco from the South) was vital to the United States.

In the decade between 1821 und 1830, America's total foreign trade amounted to 142 million dollars, 64 percent of which went to European countries. In the years following 1891, trade had increased to ten times that much, bringing yearly total American exports to 1.7 billion dollars, of which Europe received an average of 66 percent. Among America's European trading partners, Great Britain was in first place, far ahead of both France and Germany. Between 1821 and 1830, America's yearly trade average (imports and exports) amounted to 52 million dollars with Great Britain, 17 million with France and 4.7 million dollars with Germany. After 1891, these figures rose to a yearly trade balance of 610 million dollars with Great Britain, 180 million with Germany and 133 million dollars with France.

In comparison to today's volume of trade (in 1974, for example, the exchange of goods between the United States and the Federal Republic of Germany amounted to more than 12 billion dollars), earlier figures seem microscopically small. Nevertheless, proportions in trade between the two countries between 1820 and 1975 have remained fairly constant, with Germany almost always in second place among America's European trading partners. But in recent years, Germany has overtaken Great Britain and now is in first place.

The most pronounced characteristic of the similarity of interests between the two countries can be seen in the following: the continuity of German-American trade relations, the similarity of their liberal economic structures and (aside from periodic tendencies to impose tariff barriers) their mutual efforts toward freeing international trade of barriers and other impediments.

But these intensive trade relations were from the very beginning not without occasional conflicts between the two countries. They sometimes resemble the present-day controversies which arise between the United States and the European Economic Community when America believes that its agriculture is being put at a disadvantage. One need only think of the legendary "chicken war" of the middle 1960's.

When the German Tariff Union was formed under the leadership of Prussia in 1834 (something like a German "Common Market" of that time), Secretary of State John Forsyth ordered American Envoy to Berlin Henry Wheaton to "immediately and with great emphasis" take steps to get the Tariff Union partners to lower the customs duties on American tobacco and rice since cultivation of these products in the American South was being handicapped by the high tariffs. Wheaton conducted long and tedious negotiations with Prussian Finance Minister von Alvensleven. The minister insisted that customs on rice could be lowered but not on tobacco since German tobacco farmers also had a right to commercial protection. Eventually the representatives of the Tariff Union reached argreement with the American negotiator on this basis.

That initial agreement was followed by extended bargaining which eventually led to the "Wheaton Agreement" (named after the American negotiator), which was concluded in 1844 between the United States and the German Tariff Union. In this agreement, America pledged not to impose customs duties amounting to more than 20, 15 and 10 percent on three categories of agricultural and industrial products of the Tariff Union members. In return, the Tariff Union obligated itself to reduce the duties on American tobacco and lard and promised not to increase the customs on rice nor to change the regulation by which unlimited amounts of American cotton could be exported to the German states duty-free. But in the end the United States Senate refused to ratify the agreement on constitutional grounds and because of opposition from its own trade protectionists.

A prolonged controversy between the United States and the German Reich erupted in 1894. America imposed a duty charge on German sugar imports (about 15 million German marks worth of trade per year at that time) which, the Germans charged, violated the terms of reciprocity contained in the Friendship and Trade Agreement of 1828. In its internal deliberations, the American government conceded that this complaint was justified and the President recommended that the Congress retract the levy. The House of Representatives followed his recommendation but the Senate refused.

Some voices on Capitol Hill charged that Berlin had complained only in order to cover up the fact that Germany was preventing the import of American beef with the dubious claim that Texas steers were infected with a certain "fever" which made their meat detrimental to health. Indeed, on October 27, 1894, Reichs Chancellor Prince Hohenlohe had stopped the import of American beef on grounds that the cattle were suffering from "Texas Fever". The Americans protested that this illness affected animals only in certain southern states which were not allowed to export meat anyhow.

In that period, all commercial relations were determined on the one hand by preference treatment and on the other by customs duties which were levied time and time again by both nations. The relations were therefore not free of friction. At that time, American exports to Germany consisted primarily of agricultural products and raw materials such as cotton, tobacco, grain, meat, lard and eventually also oil, the price of which then was constantly falling. American imports from

Germany were made up mainly of cloth, silk, iron and steel products, paper, chemicals, glass, fashion goods, beet sugar and salt. As the two nations became industrialized, the emphasis was more and more on the exchange of manufactured goods. And before the first World War, the United States transported much of its transatlantic freight aboard German freighters.

Though political and diplomatic contacts of the two nations were at that time only of secondary importance, certain events captured the attention of people in both countries. This was particularly true of revolutionary developments in the German states between 1848 and 1849 and for the American Civil War of 1861—1865. In the middle of the century, the European nations appeared to be carrying out the same revolutionary changes (their rebellion against autocratic, feudal and monarchistic systems of government) which the Americans had already brought about through their War of Independence against the British. These revolts in Europe marked the breakthrough toward democratic government and freedom and started the Europeans on their way toward a system of equal economic opportunity for all.

Of all the European people, the Americans had expected least that the Germans would rebel. When they did, they received spontaneous, private support from Americans of important standing and the favorable disposition of official Washington.

The Americans were favorably inclined toward the German rebellion because it appeared that a permanent and not merely provisional government would emerge from the National Assembly in Frankfurt; a government which could assume the functions of the local administrations of the 39 separate German states represented at the Assembly. It seemed appropriate for the United States to get off to a timely and good start with this Central German Government for purely material reasons. The Central Government wanted to establish an all-German empire and had already appointed Archduke Johann to be Reich-Administrator. It began taking the initial steps toward achieving joint foreign and trade policies and in January, 1849, even came up with a draft for a constitution.

Washington's willingness to enter into an early relationship with the emerging German Reich was also attributable to a nationwide American inclination to favor the ideological and political goals of the German freedom movement. Dudley Mann, President James K. Polk's special envoy who negotiated trade agreements with Germany's coastal states, welcomed the revolution with the words, "After a period of 200 years following the Westphalian Peace in which the Germans apparently did little more than dream, the flag of justice has finally been unfolded." And Archduke Johann, on the other hand, told American Envoy Andrew J. Donelson, "Germany considers the United States as its best friend because both countries have the same interests and both have the desire to see the good of mankind advanced." The American Congress almost sent an official message of congratulations to the German National Assembly, but it got stuck in the Foreign Relations Committee of the House of Representatives. Nevertheless, German-Americans collected money for the victims of the March upheaval in Prussia and there certainly was no lack of congratulatory messages from private American citizens.

Envoy Donelson was willing to give the President of the Prussian National Assembly, Viktor von Unruh, political asylum in the U. S. Mission, when he was threatened by King Frederick IV, who had invoked martial law. Von Unruh, however, did not make use of this offer. This courageous though perhaps unwise act of sympathy was not exactly in keeping with protocol and almost caused a major diplomatic incident between Prussia and the United States. Less discordant was the willingness of both private and official Americans to supply the democrats in Germany and elsewhere with the texts of the American Declaration of Independence and the Constitution. These documents provided the reformers in Europe with guidelines for their ideas concerning new constitutional principles.

Washington was kept abreast of what was happening in Germany by Donelson, for a short while by Special Agent Dudley Mann as well as Charles Graebe, a German-American. As U. S. Consul in Hesse-Kassel, he reported home on both the people's rebellion of March, 1848, and the activities of the Frankfurt National Assembly. Mann even went so far as to draw up a draft proposal for a German constitution for one of his German friends. This proposal called for the creation of a "United States of Germany" patterned after the United States of America. It was based on a republican system but took into consideration the monarchic systems of rule which was to be integrated within the federation.

Other remarkable contributions to Germany's domestic deliberations on a new constitution (or comments on it) were made by Donelson in his talks with parliamentarians in Frankfurt. He reported on these talks to then-Secretary of State James Buchanan, who later became President. At the request of Baron von Gerolt (who was then Prussian envoy to Washington), conservative Senator John C. Calhoun was also active in this respect. But for the parliamentarians in Frankfurt, the American Government's willingness to recognize the Reich and to establish official diplomatic relations with it (something which Washington made very clear) was of far greater significance.

Whereas major European powers such as England, France and

Russia kept their distance from this provisional German Government and only small states like Switzerland, Belgium, Sweden, Holland, Sardinia and Naples established formal diplomatic relations with it, the United States was the first important country to offer the new government full recognition. This expression of American readiness to recognize the government was seized upon with great eagerness by the Frankfurt Government. It fully realized how important this could be for obtaining status and prestige both at home and abroad. Washington finally got the green light to go ahead with its recognition when, on June 28, 1848, the Frankfurt Constitutional Parliament (almost seven months after adopting a German Constitution) passed a law creating an executive body in which the Reich-Administrator was given authority to have the new Germany represented abroad.

On August 1, 1848, President Polk decided to have Donelson accredited as Envoy to Frankfurt, and his appointment was confirmed a few days later by the U. S. Senate. There were, however, two significant conditions for this appointment: Andrew J. Donelson was to remain Envoy to the Prussian Court and to maintain his residence in Berlin. He presented his credentials to Reich-Administrator Archduke Johann on September 15, 1848. In the accompanying letter of introduction, the United States emphasized that American interests were in no way opposed to those of Germany. Archduke Johann stressed in his reply that he needed the support of foreign countries for his activities, especially from the noble American nation.

This act by Washington corresponded fully with the American tradition of recognizing as quickly as possible new governments whose principles coincided with those of the American form of government. It required the Frankfurt Assembly some time to reciprocate by appointing an envoy to the United States. One reason for the delay was that several candidates were vying for the job. Eventually the post was given to Baron Friedrich Ludwig Rönne. He had previously represented Prussia in Washington for ten years (1834—1844) and was now to be the German Envoy to the United States. But this time he received his letter of appointment from Frankfurt.

The document arrived aboard a sailing vessel with some delay on January 24, 1849, and Baron von Rönne presented his credentials to President Polk two days later. In doing so, he stressed to the President "that now two great nations have extended their hands to each other in brotherliness." After making the customary remark concerning the principle of non-intervention in each other's affairs, Polk replied that "Germany's efforts to legally establish freedom and unity" had the full approval of the American people. Soon after taking up his duties in Washington, Rönne reported to Frankfurt that he had been received in a most friendly manner by the President, the cabinet, the Congress and by American society. "You will not easily find another country," Rönne wrote home, "that shows so much warm interest for the German cause as the United States of America."

During the short span of time before the final, violent dissolution of the provisional Central German Government and the National Assembly in the summer of 1849, the United States was especially strong in demonstrating its good will towards and, in fact, supporting outright the process of liberalization and creation of a unified state in Germany. This episode in history showed clearly under what conditions Germany can usually count on the favor and support of the United States. The exceptions were when the revolution in the German states and in Austria wandered off to the political left, in which case it lost the support of conservative circles in America and instead reaped criticism. Americans in general approved of the moderate liberal forces in Germany which (contrary to some of their American friends) did not want to go beyond the establishment of a constitutional monarchy.

The story does not end with the short-lived establishment of diplomatic relations between Frankfurt and Washington alone. The National Assembly wanted to build up a German naval force, and the idea of naval prestige was more popular among the people than many of the Assembly's other plans. What prompted the idea and made it seem reasonable was a desire to protect the German state's merchant fleet of about 5300 ships. The Marine Commission of the National Assembly approached Envoy Donelson with the request that the United States Government send a high-ranking American naval officer to Germany as an advisor. And the Assembly even contemplated having German warships built in America.

Donelson recommended to Washington that American warships be sent to the North and Baltic Seas as a demonstration of the American Government's growing interest in transatlantic trade between Germany and the United States. The first result of these efforts was the visit of the American frigate "St. Lawrence" under Captain Paulding to the North Sea in the fall of 1848. The "St. Lawrence" docked in the port of Bremerhaven on October 8th of that year.

Envoy Rönne had barely arrived in Washington when he began promoting the idea of German-American naval cooperation. The U.S. Navy expressed its interest and gave the Germans plans and blueprints for constructing warships. One of the most active American advisors was Commodore Matthew C. Perry, whose fleet was to force the opening of Japanese ports for international shipping five years later. Captain Paulding was much more reserved. In talks with the Ma-

72

rine Commission in Frankfurt he determined that the German plans for building up a navy were in part confused and in part went far beyond what Germany was capable of achieving. Paulding decisively rejected a veiled offer from Donelson that the Captain assume command of the German Navy, even though it still existed only on the drawing boards. This would have been almost impossible anyway since the American Constitution stipulates that anyone in the service of the U. S. Government cannot enter into the service of a foreign power without the explicit approval of the U. S. Congress.

Commodore Foxhall A. Parker, sent to Frankfurt at the beginning of 1849, had an even less favorable opinion of the German plans. These plans aimed primarily at purchasing an American-made warship powered by steam and at employing several officers of the U. S. Navy. Parker wrote home a report which said, "At the moment I cannot envision any task in the German Navy for an American officer that would bring honor to either him or his country." The complete inferiority of the German Navy compared with that of Denmark (as demonstrated in the newly-erupting conflicts between the two countries adjacent to both the North and Baltic Seas) may well have prompted Parker to make this judgement. In any case, President Polk let envoy Rönne know that it would be unfeasible to have American naval officers serving in the German Navy.

This plan, which originally had been met with enthusiasm on both sides, in the end caused friction between Frankfurt and Washington. Nevertheless, indefatigable Rönne at least succeeded in pushing through the purchase of the side-wheeler steamship "United States" from New York for about $ 397,000 and had it converted into a warship brandishing twelve cannons. He was also able to recruit for it an American crew under the command of Merchant Marine Captain Nathaniel B. Palmer. In addition he managed to get three American citizens to vouch for a $ 600,00 security bond which the American Government—concerned about maintaining its neutrality—had demanded be put up for the ship and conversion work.

On May 31, 1849, the "United States" steamed out of New York harbor flying the black-red-gold flag of the provisional Frankfurt Government. After a turbulent crossing, she reached Liverpool. German Captain J. O. Donner took command of the vessel in England and in August of that year sailed her into the Weser River. There, the ship was rechristened and given the name "Hansa". But the "Hansa" never saw active service as part of a German Reich Navy.

In the summer of 1849, the Frankfurt National Assembly was dissolved by force. The German fleet was put up for auction in 1852. The "Hansa" was sold from one Bremen shipping company to another and for several years steamed across the Atlantic transporting cargo. And that was the inglorious end of the promising beginnings of German-American naval cooperation in the middle of the last century.

Looking at history from the other side, in Germany (and especially in Prussia) there was an almost spontaneous enthusiasm for the American North when the Civil War (1861—1865) erupted. Many Germans applied for service in the Union Army. It came to the point where the American Envoy in Berlin was forced to post the following sign on the door of his office building: "This is not a recruiting office!"

A private American citizen had written to Secretary of State William H. Seward from Berlin that in the summer of 1862 many Prussian soldiers were due to be released from military service. He suggested that if they were provided with free transportation to the United States, thousands of well-trained soldiers could be absorbed into the Union Army. But Seward turned down this proposal saying, "This government cannot possibly make available special services to the subjects of foreign powers in order to get them to enter the service of the armies of the United States without causing a scandal. And besides, it would be even more difficult for it to pay them." During the Civil War the Prussian Government—if only for the sake of being on the side of legitimacy—clearly favored the Union and did not give any support to the secessionist South, which Prussia viewed as a "revolutionary" movement.

Prussia's position during the Civil War was not forgotten by the victors, who were one day to reciprocate. Immediately after the war between France and Germany broke out in 1870, President Ulysses S. Grant issued a proclamation of neutrality. Bismarck, for his part, made it known that any private American property on the high seas would not be touched by Prussian warships. That received wide and lively approval from Americans. During the German-French war, the United States Embassy in Paris took care of German interests, such as protecting Germans and their property.

But the United States did not try to mediate between the two warring countries because Germany would not have gone along with this anyway. Secretary of State Hamilton Fish even avoided making any statement on the German-French peace conditions since, as he explained, both nations "enjoy the friendship of the United States equally." But immediately after the fall of Napoleon III, the United States recognized the newly-established republican French Government. This, indeed, prompted some indignation in Berlin.

At that time relations between Germany and America were almost completely unclouded. Both powers had demonstrated their mutual friendship and trust through numerous small reciprocal acts of

74

diplomatic assistance. The United States for a while looked after German interests also in Peru and even mediated in pushing through some German property claims. In the summer of 1871 (together with the British government), the United States requested the services of German Emperor William I to mediate in a particularly touchy matter of contention over which Washington and London had waged a ten-year dispute: determining the official border between the United States and British Canada in the northwest section of Puget Sound and, above all, the question of who owned the group of San Juan Islands north of that.

On September 1, 1871, the German Emperor officially accepted the role as mediator. In December, the two opposing parties submitted their memoranda outlining their claims. William I called in a panel of authorities composed of three legal experts: Dr. Ferdinand Grimm, Dr. Levin Goldschmid and Professor Heinrich Kiepert. They immediately began closed-door consultations and studied the matter with German thoroughness for almost a full year.

On September 30, 1872, they presented their 35-page expertise containing two differing opinions. The monarch backed the majority of Grimm and Kiepert and made the following decision: "The claim of the Government of the United States of America that the borderline between the territories of Her British Majesty and those of the United States should be drawn through the Haro Channel is most in line with a correct interpretation of the treaty dated Washington, June 15, 1846, concluded between the Governments of Her British Majesty and the United States of America. Signed, Berlin, October 21, 1872, Wilhelm."

Thus the 172 islands making up the San Juan Archipel became unquestionably the possession of the United States. Today, thanks to the remaining relics of English and American military installations and to their beautiful landscape, the islands are a popular tourist attraction. A large portrait of Prince Bismarck now hanging in a public building of Friday Harbor on San Juan Island serves as a memorial to the German mediation.

The founding of the German Reich and the final settlement of the American West predestined the two nations to enter the age of imperialism even before the turn of the century. This age was marked by the acquisition of overseas territories (colonies or protectorates) and the assembly of powerful fleets to keep the shipping routes open. This for the first time led to German-American military friction, such as the repeated crises over Samoa and the differences of opinion concerning the influence the two countries should have in China. But these events were still far removed from the tensions which were to bring about the first World War in Europa in 1914 and American's entrance into the war in 1917 on the side of the western Entente. The minor impairments of German-American relations mentioned above were, however, symptoms which farsighted statesmen should have considered as warnings.

When German Chancellor Prince Otto von Bismarck was dismissed by ambitious and impulsive Emperor William II in 1890, Germany's policy of carefully maintaining a balance of power between Russia and Austria began to crumble; European alliances began to take shape. In Germany (at least as far as public political consciousness was concerned), it had gone unnoticed that in the first decade of the 20th century the United States had become the greatest industrial power in the world.

The United States, Great Britain and Germany were all simultaneously involved in the conflict over Samoa, a group of islands 3,000 miles south of Hawaii in a position to dominate the sea lanes through the southern Pacific Ocean. Between 1872 and 1878, America had procured preference on Samoa through a treaty with a native prince. The two other powers tried to contest this by also concluding agreements with local notables. For a good ten years, Washington, London and Berlin played off their native protégés against one another. This went on until 1889, when the simultaneous appearance of American, British and German warships in Samoan waters threatened to cause a military incident.

Since the Germans did not want to spoil their relations with America, they invited the United States and England to a mediation conference in Berlin. This ended with an agreement on the establishment of a three-power protectorate for the Samoa Islands. This did not prove to be a durable solution and in 1899 the United States and Germany divided up the islands between themselves and gave the British compensation elsewhere in the Pacific.

After the United States had taken possession of the Philippines in the war with Spain in 1898, and Presidents William McKinley and Theodore Roosevelt had pursued aggressive expansionist policies, the United States turned its attention more and more to the Asiatic mainland. America had now become a Pacific power. Since the middle of the 19th century, the European powers had procured for themselves special rights on the Chinese mainland by virtue of a number of "unequal treaties" which threatened to exclude other countries from trade with China. American opposition to this was directed against any establishment of spheres of influence, not specifically against the actions of the Germans. They, after all, had made themselves particularly conspicuous by crushing the "Boxer-Rebellion" of 1900 and through William II's inflamatory speeches about "the yellow peril".

In late 1899, John Hay, Secretary of State in the McKinley Administration, demanded that all colonial powers which had a foothold in China agree to an "open door policy" in that area. His proposal was that all countries with spheres of influence in China should respect the rights of other powers and not discriminate against them by imposing harbor taxes on their ships or special levies on their railway freight. Russia rejected this proposal; the other Europeans—England, Germany, France and Italy—and also Japan gave evasive replies. It was only after the "Boxer-Rebellion" that Hay succeeded in obtaining Germany's and England's consent to his proposal. This proposal was by then, however, no longer confined to the interest spheres of foreign powers; it applied to the entire Chinese Empire.

Emperor Wilhelm II strived for German naval power and underestimated the "special relationship" between Great Britain and the USA

Notwithstanding the overall peaceful and good-neighborly nature of these events, the naval buildup of the two nations had sown the seeds for real German-American rivalry. William II's intensification of shipbuilding was directed against Britain's naval superiority as defined in Great Britain's "Two-Power Standard": The British fleet should always be stronger than the combined fleets of the next two strongest navies in the world. But just as William II, President Theodore Roosevelt was anxious to make the American Navy impressive and second in strength only to the British fleet. This American naval buildup was, however, not directed so much against Great Britain. It was an instrument to secure American supremacy in the Western Hemisphere and to shield US interests in the Far East. Subsequently US naval power gained weight against the German Reich with its growing political and economic influence in Central and South America.

The armaments race was in full swing around 1905, while in Europe the constellation of power was heading more and more toward an inevitable collision. In 1906, America achieved its goal of becoming the world's mightiest naval power second only to Great Britain. But a few years later, the United States was pushed into third place by Germany.

America and Germany had had their first major dispute in 1903, when the Germans (together with the Italians) imposed a blockade on Venezuela and fired on its harbor to collect a bad debt. Teddy Roosevelt later claimed that he had let the German government know that the United States would answer any attempt by a foreign nation to take possession of territories in the Western Hemisphere with gunfire. Berlin eventually did, indeed, give in and agreed to have its dispute with Venezuela over its debts settled by arbitration.

But fears remained alive in the United States that the German Reich might have ambitions in Central and South America going as far as wanting to take possession of territory. And for the first time, American-German relations had changed from trust to distrust. In the same period, 1903 to be exact, America's relations with England, on the other hand, were so smooth and cordial that the British withdrew almost their entire naval forces from the Caribbean, thereby turning over control of the area to the United States Navy.

5
Enemies become Allies

Since the beginning of the 20th century, humanity has existed in an unpeaceful state. Between 1914 and 1975, there have been two armed global conflicts, many other declared and undeclared wars, civil wars, revolutions and innumerable military coups. Entire social classes and aristocracies have been swept away or mercilessly exterminated in the course of violent social upheavals. One need only recall the Bolshevik Revolution in Russia, the communist victories in China and other countries. The racist insanity of Hitlerism brought about the first systematic extermination of a large ethnic and religiously homogeneous group—the Jews in Europe—by a country which until then had been considered to be exceptionally civilized and cultured.

Decolonialization and rapid scientific and technological progress have set new elementary forces into motion and simultaneously have widened the productivity gap between the Northern and Southern Hemispheres considerably. Atavistic drives motivated by greed and power, gross differences between rich and poor and differing social systems competing with each other created untold new areas of tension. An accumulation of horrifying ways and means of destruction in the atomic age awakens dark visions of the dangers of an inferno on this earth. United Nations Secretary General Kurt Waldheim estimates that since 1945, more than twenty million persons have been the victims of small conflicts.

Germany and America collided with each other in both global conflicts; the first and second World Wars. Both times many Americans believed that they were going off to fight the "war to end all wars". But that, as we know, was an illusion. America was to become entangled in new military ventures in which the Germans were not involved and which sometimes brought the United States to the brink of an especially dangerous situation: in Korea, in Indochina, in the Berlin blockade, in the Cuban missile crisis and the numerous encounters between Arabs and Israelis.

As a consequence of the two World Wars, many Americans formed a cliché opinion of the losers: Germans are aggressive and militaristic. Popular American authors did their part to perpetuate the belief that aggressiveness and militarism could well be unchangeable traits of the German character; traits which had made themselves apparent in the characters of all significant figures in German history from Martin Luther to Adolf Hitler. Since the barbaric deeds of "the Germans" under the Nazis in the Third Reich provided almost inexhaustible nourishment for such a view of history, a widespread generalization found in America is that the Germans have a blemished character of sorts.

Historians generally agree that Germany under Kaiser Wilhelm II was partially though not solely responsible for the outbreak of World War I. Other nations and their leaders share this responsibility; Europe literally stumbled into this conflict.

Indeed, all European states have waged wars against one another at one time in history. And up to Napoleon I, it was the Germans who in fact were more often the victims of aggression and intervention than their neighbors. Other peoples were no less barbaric than the Germans. Germany's central geographic location and its late start in becoming a European nation-state were major factors which contributed to Germany often being involved in armed conflicts.

Germany did not willfully seek the two wars with the United States. In fact in the periods immediately after 1914 and 1939, the German governments were intent on avoiding a collision with America. But in both cases, willful or not, the policies pursued by those governments were without a doubt provocations for America. Berlin underestimated both America's interest in Europe and its military and economic potential. But even Adolf Hitler, notorious for his lack of selfcontrol, instructed his naval commanders to avoid military confrontations with American forces. These orders remained in effect until the Japanese attacked Pearl Harbor and Hitler declared war on the United States on December 11, 1941. And his widely-publicized propaganda attacks and hate tirades against the American President and people do not alter these facts.

America's resistance to boundless German expansion and Washington's support of the Western Allies were hardly coincidental. Presidents Woodrow Wilson and Franklin D. Roosevelt acted in full accordance with America's own security and political interests when they led the United States to the front of Germany's adversaries. In the first World War, the United States adopted as its policy the principle which had guided the British as a seafaring power and had prompted England one hundred years earlier to battle Napoleon I: to prevent with all means necessary that a single country rule Continental Europe.

Franklin Roosevelt's intervention in Europe was prompted by the larger dimensions of the conflict. The war unleashed by Hitler against

Germany's European neighbors took on global proportions with the Japanese attacks on European colonial possessions in Asia and against the United States. The war went beyond the nature of a pure power conflict because the axis powers were governments with similar totalitarian systems. They did not only want to divide the world among themselves but also to establish a "New Order" in keeping with their philosphies.

An additional and distinctive feature of the two German-American conflicts is the generosity with which the United States treated its enemy once he had been brought to his knees. After the second World War, existing world political conditions were such that West Germany even became a close ally of the United States. But quite aside from this development resulting from the postwar "cold war" power struggle between the Soviet Union and the United States (which eventually led to West Germany's inclusion in NATO), the Americans twice helped the conquered Germans back on their feet with enormous amounts of humanitarian aid as well as political and economic support. It was essential for Germany after 1918 and decisive after 1945.

The United States fought its two wars against Germany with heavy moral overtones. Quite in keeping with this conviction that America had a missionary calling, General Dwight D. Eisenhower even entitled his war memoirs *"Crusade in Europe"*. But the morality felt by the United States did not end once it had been victorious: America demonstrated considerable and farsighted generosity in the treatment of its vanquished enemy.

The United States was not able to establish a "just peace" in Europe either in 1918 or in 1945. But it is indisputable that in their treatment of their conquered German adversaries, the Americans did not succumb to what must have been a strong temptation to seek revenge; this did, in fact, occur to some American politicians. And history shows that in this respect, the Americans were pleasantly and distinctively different as victors when compared with the traditional behavior of most European nations, including the Germans.

When the first world war broke out following the murder of the successor to the Austrian throne, Franz Ferdinand, on June 28, 1914, at Sarajevo, the American people were completely unprepared for the new situation. The deeper causes of the conflict between the Central Powers—Germany, Austria-Hungary, Bulgaria and Turkey—and the Entente Powers—Russia, France, Great Britain and eventually also Italy—remained so incomprehensible and obscure to the American people that even as late as 1916 President Wilson described this war as "a drunken brawl in a public house" and proclaimed American neutrality.

In the early stages of the war confined to the Continent, American public opinion was divided. German-Americans and circles sympathizing with the Germans tried to make their countrymen believe that Kaiser Wilhelm was waging a defensive war which was also directed against the autocracy of czarist Russia. But from the very beginning, the sympathies of the educated classes in America lay with the Entente Powers, especially with Great Britain and France.

This was the first war accompanied and supported by the mass media which succeeded in setting off the first wave to public outrage in America through reports on alleged atrocities in Belgium. The Germans clumsily tried to influence world opinion with their entirely unconvincing argument that they had been "encircled" by the alliance policies of France and Russia.

Even though the Allies were able to make deeper and deeper inroads into American sympathy, the first years following 1914 did not produce any American inclination to give up U.S. neutrality. The war appeared to be an exclusively European conflict not affecting the United States. But gradually the events of the war and their indirect effects on the United States prompted a change in this thinking. And it was not long before Wilson's declaration of neutrality became outdated. The United States was no longer an onlooker; it was feeling the effects of the trade war which Great Britain and Germany were waging on the Atlantic, the British with their total blockade of the Central Powers and the Germans with their submarine attacks on Allied shipping.

Since the English controlled the open waters with their superior fleet, the blockade seriously affected America's agricultural export trade with Central Europe. American exports to Germany and Austria (which had been about 170 million dollars before the ware began) soon dropped to almost zero. And even though, for example, cotton was not among the items on the first British contraband list, the English refused to let this type of cargo pass to Europe. Some weak protests from President Wilson did not change this.

As trade between America and the Germans and Austrians died, it began to flourish with the Entente Powers in hitherto unknown quantities: it rose from 824 million dollars in 1914 to 3,1 billion dollars in 1916. As early as March of 1915, the American government eased the severe restrictions on borrowing by the Entente Powers in the United States. So, long before it officially entered the war, America was involved in the conflict economically and financially—on the side of the English and French.

In the beginning, Germany was able to make great but not decisive military gains in the west. Germany's victories over Russia eventually led to the collapse of the Czarist Empire. But before this touched off the Bolshevist Revolution under Wladimir Iljitsch Lenin—whom the Germans permitted to travel from Switzerland to Finland—, the Central European powers became aware of the danger that they would be strangled by the effective British blockade. Germany's response was its submarine offensive.

This put the Germans in the dilemma of not being able to adhere to international laws governing the capture and sinking of ships and simultaneously wanting to wage this type of warfare. The extremely slow and vulnerable "U-boats" would have invited their own demise by first surfacing to capture and then sink a cargo vessel which might be protected by a warship hovering somewhere nearby. Consequently, the German government decided that as of February 4, 1915, enemy vessels found in an area around the British Isles, declared by Berlin to be a war zone, would be sunk without advance warning.

This set the stage for inevitable incidents between Germany and the United States, which soon occured. Americans often were among the victims of German attacks on British passenger liners. The first recorded death of a U.S. citizen was that of Leon C. Thrasher, who drowned when the "Falaba" was sunk on March 28, 1915. But soon German torpedoes were also being aimed at American cargo ships, causing, however, only minor casualties.

The sinking of the "Lusitania" by a German submarine in 1915 with losses of American lives stirred anti-German sentiments in the USA

It was not long, however, before the tragedy occured which raised a furor in America: At 2:15 p.m. on May 7, 1915, the German submarine "U-20" torpedoed the British Cunard Line passenger ship "Lusitania" off the coast of Ireland without advance warning. Of the 1,153 passengers, 783 lost their lives; among them 128 Americans. In the dispute which this tragedy touched off, the Germans claimed that the "Lusitania" had been transporting ammunition, was armed with camouflaged cannons and in reality had been an auxiliary cruiser of the British Admiralty. The Allies, for their part, cited a warning the German Embassy had placed in ad-form in a newspaper as proof that the attack had been pre-planned. It read: "... travelers sailing in the war zone on ships of Great Britain and her allies do so at their own risk."

But what was decisive and most welcome to the British was the psychological effect of this tragedy. An outcry of indignation over this act of "uncivilized warfare" went up from all sides in America. This incident and those which soon followed prompted a series of increasingly harsh American protests in Berlin intended to force Germany to stop its submarine warfare. But the United States intervened against the total British blockade of trade with Central Europe with only mild and futile protests. And this in itself indicated clearly where America really stood in the conflict. Nevertheless, Germany gave in temporarily to the American pressure and assured Washington that it would no longer sink passenger liners without warning.

The tensions, however, subsided for but a short time. When in 1916 the Allies began to arm their cargo vessels and ordered them to fire on German submarines on sight, the German government answered by resuming its torpedoing of such ships. When the English Channel passenger ship "Sussex" was sunk, several Americans were on bord. Now the American government reacted in a more threatening tone. On April 18, 1916, Secretary of State Robert Lansing sent the following note to Berlin:

"Unless the Imperial Government should not immediately declare and effect an abandonment of its present methods of submarine warfare against passenger and freight-carrying vessels, the Government of the United States can have no choice but to sever diplomatic relations with the German Empire altogether."

Once again—and this time for the last time—the Germans yielded and gave Washington new assurances that they would respect the rules of marine warfare with regard to stop-and-search of vessels.

But developments leading to outright war could no longer be stemmed, even though President Wilson tried to mediate all the way up to the end of 1916. In fact, on January 22, 1917, he went before the U.S. Senate to appeal for a "peace without victory" which would take the following shape: disarmament, the right of selfdetermination for all peoples and the creation of a League of Nations in which the United States would participate in securing international peace. But Chancellor of the German Reich Bethmann Hollweg was not able to prevail against Germany's generals and admirals. They wanted the taste of outright victory.

In this decisive moment, the Imperial Government committed what probably was the most severe error in Berlin's dealings with the United States since the beginning of the war: on January 31, 1917, in the midst of Wilson's peace offensive, Germany declared "unrestricted submarine warfare" on the high seas. From the next day on, Berlin warned, every ship found in the wide blockaded zone around the British Isles and France and in parts of the Mediterannean would be attacked und sunk without advance warning and regardless of whether it was flying an enemy or neutral flag. Only once a week, the declaration continued, will one ship—clearly identifiable as being American—be permitted to dock at the British harbor of Falmouth, provided it not carry contraband. The peace terms which Germany offered in the declaration were completely unacceptable to the Allies; they were tantamount to surrender.

America meanwhile had begun to prepare for war. Germany's proclamation of unrestricted submarine warfare left President Wilson no choice other than to act, especially considering growing anti-German public sentiment and increasing pressure from Congress. On February 3, 1917, the United States broke diplomatic relations with the German Reich. In his memoirs, Count Johann-Heinrich von Bernstorff, Germany's Ambassador to the United States, had the following to say about his government's actions:

"On January 19th I received official notification that unrestricted submarine warfare would begin on the first of February ... Considering all that had transpired up to then, I could but only regard this message as a declaration of war on the United States; an act which put us entirely in the wrong since it threw overboard the peace offensive which Mr. Wilson had undertaken with our consent."

Count Bernstorff tried unsuccessfully to get Berlin to postpone these measures which, in his opinion, could only lead to catastrophe. And after German submarines had sunk four American cargo ships one right after the other in March, his prediction came true. Wilson now had no choice. Anti-German sentiment in the United States had meanwhile exceeded the boiling point, partially as a reaction to the publication of a note from German Foreign Minister Arthur Zimmermann to the German Envoy to Mexico.

This note (which the British had been able to intercept) was a revelation of the utmost stupidity of German diplomacy. It proposed that should a German-American war begin, Mexico should also become hostile toward the United States and use the opportunity to try to reconquer the former Mexican territories in California, Texas and New Mexico which had been annexed by America. Japan, which was in fact at war with Germany, should—the note suggested—be included in this strange alliance. On April 2, 1917, President Wilson asked Congress to declare war on the Central Powers, and four days later Congress complied.

The United States was now actively participating in the bloody struggle in Europe. There were a number of reasons for America's entry into the conflict. The primary reason was neutral America's narrow interpretation of maritime law, which was no longer in keeping with technical advances that had been made in warfare. But other more objective factors actually triggered America's decision to join the fight. In the spring of 1917, the two Western Allies were down in their strength. The German submarines were destroying up to 900,000 tons of shipping a month and the French armies were marked by defeatism and mutiny. America was thus faced with the choice of either allowing France and England to be defeated or helping them. It was this situation which turned Americans emotionally against Germany, and which determined Washington's course of action.

America's entry into the war did not immediately change the situation on the battlefields. But it had a decisive psychological and political effect on both sides. From that moment on, the two Western Allies knew that they would have the full support of America's enormous industrial capacity. This meant that they would no longer lose the war, and their fighting morale received a tremendous boost.

The Germans, on the other hand, were dealt a severe psychological blow. They were now faced with a much more powerful enemy. The battle experience of American soldiers was not considered up to par by the Germans, but the highly-experienced German generals soon were to be impressed by the amounts of material and equipment the United States would roll up to the front.

America's participation in the war was first felt on the Atlantic. In the summer of 1917, the German submarines had been sinking three times as many cargo ships as the Allies were building. But now America came to the rescue: before the war ended, the United States had ship tonnage amounting to nine million afloat on the Atlantic, including half a million tons launched especially for the war effort.

The convoy system of sailing (which the United States put into practice against the advice of the British) eventually halted the German submarine campaign. Between April 6, 1917, and November 11, 1918 (the day of the armistice), two million soldiers were transported to Europe (half of them on British ships) to serve in the "American Expeditionary Forces". Not a single troop transporting ship was lost in the Atlantic.

At the peak of the military campaign, there were 42 American divisions in France. Each division had 27,000 men. The U.S. Navy adapted to the new situation by concentrating on the construction of destroyers and submarine-chasers. This enabled the United States to span "a protected bridge of ships" across the Atlantic which secured the supply of food, material and equipment for the Western Allies and the American Expeditionary Forces.

The presence of American soldiers in Europe really made itself felt at the beginning of 1918. Until then, and at the outbreak of the war, there had been no American land forces worth mentioning. But soon the Americans began to move, and by the fall of 1918, 29 of America's 42 divisions were at the front, holding 101 miles of it. This was even slightly more front territory than the British were holding. At the beginning of the war, the American soldiers had been fairly inexperienced in combat. But it was not long until they demonstrated a lively fighting spirit under General John J. Pershing and the command of Allied generals.

Following the outbreak of the October Revolution in Russia and the start of German-Soviet peace negotiations, the German General Staff delegated its forces to the western front for the final and decisive offensive. In May of 1918, the Germans unleashed their assault across the Marne at Chateau-Thierry. Two months later, the Germans tried to break through the French lines at Reims. The Americans contributed heavily to holding the line in both battles. They also played a major role in the Allied counter-offensive and 47-day struggle through the Argonne Forest. This began on September 26, 1918, and turned out to be one of the bloodiest confrontations of the war. Two weeks later, on November 7, the American soldiers fought their way to Sedan, establishing the first Allied bridgeheads on the opposite banks of the Mosel River.

On November 11, 1918, the Germans accepted the armistice conditions presented by the Commander in Chief of the Allied Forces, French Marshal Ferdinand Foch. The first World War had ended. The outcome had been decided by American participation. American losses: 125,000 dead (50,300 on the battlefield, the others from illness) and 206,000 wounded.

The sacrifices which this war had demanded in terms of human beings and material was shocking: around ten million soldiers (1.8

million Germans) died on the battlefields; more than twenty million were wounded. The total cost was 186 billion dollars; the Western Allies spent 123 billion, the Central Powers 63 billion. The cost to America in terms of money was approximately 35 billion dollars, of which 8.8 billion were debts owed by the Entente governments. They paid back only about one-fourth of this amount.

The political effects of the first World War were on the same level as the costs, at least as far as severity was concerned. Czarism was destroyed in Russia and communists took control of the largest country on earth. The Austrian-Hungarian monarchy disintegrated and tiny new states emerged in eastern Europe, thereby dissolving the old balance of power system in Central Europe. The German Reich was no longer either a colonial nor a seafaring power, but despite some territorial losses and large reparation payments was able to maintain the basis for a new rise to the status of a major power. Great Britain lost its naval two-power-standard and together with France was facing the loss of its colonial empire. The Continental European Western Allies who had been victorious, did not want to face it but eventually came to realize that there had been no winners in Europe, only losers.

If there had been a winner at all, then it was the United States. Participation in the war had forced the American economy into an unprecedented boom. The United States was no longer an indebted nation, it was now a creditor. America had become the leading power in the world. It was able to influence the fate of Europe.

The United States entered into the peace negotiations with about the same amount of enthusiasm and determination that it had when it stepped into the war which was supposed to bring peace and a new balance of power to Europe. President Wilson's government had not set precise goals for the war and had outlined them only vaguely in the "fourteen points" he listed in his famous speech to Congress on January 8, 1918. But the two main Entente powers, France and Great Britain, knew quite well what *they* wanted to achieve at a peace conference. When it began in Versailles, French Premier Georges ("The Tiger") Clemenceau turned out to be the strongest, pitiless and most determined proponent of a "peace by dictate" by which Germany was to be kept in check for a long time to come. Neither Woodrow Wilson nor the other two main figures of "the big four" at the Versailles Conference (British Prime Minister David Lloyd George and Italy's Chief of Government Vittorio Orlando) were a match for Georges Clemenceau.

The monarchy in Germany had been overthrown by the revolution. Wilhelm II had sought asylum in Holland and a democratic government led by Social Democrat Friedrich Ebert as President of the Reich had

Big Four at Versailles: Orlando (Italy), Lloyd George (Great Britain), Clemenceau (France) and President Woodrow Wilson (from left to right)

been installed in Germany. For these reasons, the defeated Germans hoped that Wilson's "fourteen points" would form the basis for negotiations. In addition to proposing freedom of movement on the seas, worldwide disarmament and impartial adjustment of all colonial claims, Wilson's points called for the right to selfdetermination for all nations and the creation of a League of Nations.

But what remained of the fourteen points (with which Wilson had obtained the greatest imaginable backing from liberal groups all over the world) were only those guidelines of principle which concurred with the goals of the Entente Powers: self-determination freed the east Europeans and other former subjects of the Reich and of Austria, but was in no way applied to three million Germans living in the Sudeten territories of Czechoslovakia and ethnic Germans inhabiting the border areas of Poland.

In the Treaty of Versailles, the Western Allies forced Germany to accept sole responsibility for the war. And on the basis of this guilt, the Allies laid their claims to what at first were demands for unlimited German reparation payments. The U.S. Senate refused to go along with American membership in the League of Nations. Germany was excluded from membership for many years by the western European powers. This international organization was therefore gradually transformed from an instrument for securing peace into a not even well-camouflaged vehicle for securing French-British hegemony in Europe, at least in the initial years of its existence.

What remained of Wilson's proposal for general disarmament was the unilateral demilitarization of Germany and a limitation of its troop strength to a mere 100,000 men. But as a professional army, this "Reichswehr" soon became a state within the state and was the secret protector of many reactionaries in Germany.

Thus, "Adolf Hitler was born in Versailles," as one of his German contemporaries once said quite aptly. Seen retrospectively, the 21 years of peace between 1918 and the outbreak of World War II were but a prolonged armistice. The connection between the two wars is quite apparent. The developments which came after Versailles could only have been prevented if the United States had pushed through some sort of modus vivendi between Germany, France and Great Britain. Admittedly, this would have required a great desire for reconciliation on the part of the two Entente Powers, after the horrible four years they had just been through. But President Wilson was neither sufficiently familiar with European conditions nor did he have enough determination or elbow-room to insist on a durable solution.

Despite these shortcomings, however, Wilson (with cooperation from Lloyd George) was able to hinder Clemenceau's plans for dividing up Germany into buffer states. As questionable as the American President's diplomatic efforts in Versailles were, he was undisputed in his reputation in Europe as a peace dove with only the highest of intentions. The peoples of Europe considered him intent on bringing democracy, justice and peace to the Continent.

The U.S. Senate refused to ratify the Treaty of Versailles because of the planned American membership in the League of Nations. Instead, the United States concluded its own peace treaty with Germany on August 25, 1921 in Berlin. In addition to re-establishing peace between the two countries, the agreement excluded the war-responsibility clause and all of the territorial and other punishments contained in the Versailles document, but maintained the treaty's financial and economic provisions.

There had been considerable criticism of Wilson in Germany (even in moderate and Social Democratic circles) because of the discrepancies between his "fourteen points" and what came out of the Versailles negotiations. But these critics praised the German-American peace treaty as a significant step in the right direction, especially since it had been negotiated as between equal partners and with neither side forcing its will on the other.

America profited greatly from German wealth it confiscated within its own borders and from exploiting the German patents—especially in the chemical industry-which it had secured during the war. But in the period following Versailles, the United States demonstrated far-sightedness and realism on the vital question of reparations, especially in comparison to France. Washington recognized more quickly than the Europeans themselves had the need for re-establishing healthy economic conditions on the Continent. America realized that continuing rivalries stemming from the war would have to be channeled for productive purposes and eliminated altogether if a new catastrophe was to be averted. Indeed, American diplomacy (which had often caused Europeans to smirk because of its occasional amateurishness and its missionary motives) demonstrated much more awareness of its responsibilities in introducing measures geared to maintain peace than most European statesmen.

The human trait of the American character made itself felt in spontaneous and generous assistance to Germans who were starving as a result of the British blockade, which remained in effect even after the armistice. The Germans and other Central and East European nations were given mostly food. The man who was in charge of seeing to it that the goods got to Europe was Herbert Hoover, the future President of the United States. Private and religious charitable organizations were also involved in the campaign to feed Europe. Many Germans alive today still recall quite vividly how in the years following 1918 they were given "Quaker food" from America in school every day. The meal consisted of a glass of cocoa and a roll spread with real butter; things which many a German youngster had never tasted up to then.

America's position on the question of reparation payments—which was to become a vicious circle—was of utmost importance. An Allied Reparations Commission was assigned the task of determining the final amount of reparation payments Germany would have to make. But even before the Commission had set an upper limit, the Western powers began ruthlessly to collect tangible goods and cash from the Germans. Since the two continental Western Powers themselves had huge war debts to pay to the United States, Paris and London tried to tie the amounts of German reparation to the payments they had to make to Washington. But the American government stubbornly and consistently refused to go along with this.

The bleeding German economy had been weakened by the war, the occupation of the industrial Ruhr Valley and Rhineland areas and revolts from the extreme left and right which almost reached the proportions of civil war. The economy would have collapsed altogether if it had not been for the help of private American banks. They gave medium and long-term credits amounting to several hundred million dollars to German industry and communities. In fact, it was these loans that made possible a stabilization of German currency and the regeneration of an economy which had almost been entirely ruined by rampant inflation. But the reparations payments hung like a lead weight around the neck of the German economy. And politically they were the best ammunition (alongside Hitler's racist theories and the discriminating clauses in the Treaty of Versailles) the National Socialists could have hoped for to illustrate their propaganda campaign against the alleged "enslavement of the German people".

In the end, it was the Americans who pushed through gradual (but none the less substantial) alleviation of Germany's reparations burden. In 1931, President Hoover declared a moratorium on German reparation payments and the repayment of war debts by the Allies to the United States in view of the growing economic depression in the western world. His Secretary of State, Henry L. Stimson, was in favor of cancelling the debts entirely. But Hoover intended to give Germany and the Allies only temporary reprieve and limited the moratorium to one year.

At a conference of the European Powers in Lausanne, Switzerland, the following year, it was decided that Germany's total final reparations debt should be three billion Reich marks. But the German payments to the victorious powers and the payments of the Allied war debts to the United States stopped altogether before the end of 1932. The only exception was Finland, which met its obligations down to the last penny.

Nevertheless, the reparation problem ramained the heaviest burden on Germany's relations with its western neighbors until 1932. At the beginning of the 1930's (which found the world entering into a worldwide economic crisis and a period of mass unemployment—in Germany alone almost six million were jobless—), the reparation payments provided Hitler's demagogic attacks with the plausible examples he needed for inflaming the masses and getting them on his side. With cunning deliberateness, the Nazi propaganda machine attacked America's reasonable and moderate reparations policy, which in fact was aimed at a step-by-step reduction of the exaggerated demands being made by France and Great Britain. Instead of acknowledging this, the Nazis pounded the American officials doing the tedious work intended to ease Germany's burden. To a not very well-informed German public, it was easy for the Nazis to denounce U.S. Reparations Agent Gilbert Parker and American bankers Owen D. Young and General Charles G. Dawes as buzzards and hyenas trying to plunder Germany.

The magnitude of the reparation problem and its political repercussions must be seen against the background of the overall financial burden Germany was bearing as a result of its defeat. In addition to the reparation payments, one must consider the deliveries of German goods, the surrender of its cargo vessels, the confiscation of private and state-owned German property abroad. The estimates of the Allied Reparations Commission and the German government concerning the total value of this vary considerably. According to Allied calculations, until they stopped meeting their obligations in 1932, the Germans had given up goods and services totaling 20.7 billion marks. German calculations, however, put the amount at 68.6 billion. *)

Until the payments stopped because the Lausanne Agreement was never put into effect, the reparations and America's demands on its Allied debtors caused a series of disputes. On the one hand, America wanted to have its financial claims on England, France and Italy satisfied and on the other to get them to agree to a reasonable settlement of their claims on Germany. One idea behind this was to prevent a collapse of Germany's budget and its balance of payments. This would have had a damaging effect on the entire world economy.

In accordance with the Dawes Plan of 1924, the American reparations policy was more or less calculated to initially support Germany's currency with a loan of about 200 million dollars. Then, soon afterwards, the German Reich was to begin making annual payments of approximately 2.4 billion gold marks taken partly from the budget and partly from the income of the German railroads and industry. Foreign Minister Gustav Stresemann welcomed the Dawes Plan as a suitable instrument for solving the reparations problem in a manner which would be bearable for Germany. But the commitments foreseen by

---

*) One U.S. dollar was worth approximately four gold marks, annuity marks or Reich marks. The exchange rate fluctuated only slightly. In 1949, the dollar was being exchanged for 4.40 Deutsch marks. Since the dollar devaluation and the mark revaluations after 1970, the American currency has lost much of its value in comparison to the mark. In 1975, the dollar's average exchange rate in Germany was approximately 2.50 Deutsch marks.

the plan turned out to surpass Germany's financial capabilities and it was therefore replaced in 1930 by the Young Plan.

This new plan called for lower annual reparation payments. But with all obligations put together, Germany would still have had to pay 2.3 billion marks annually through 1965 and then continue meeting various financial obligations through March 31, *1988*! Under the Young Plan, the total German debt (including interest) was 113.9 billion Reich marks, of which 28.7 billion were outright reparations payments. Right after the war the Entente Powers had demanded reparations alone amounting to 226 billion gold marks. Nevertheless, the amount called for in the Young Plan and the duration of the payments were the primary propaganda targets of the "National Opposition" led by Hitler and supported by conservative parties.

Even though the problem of German payments to the Allies and the United States (whose demands were relatively modest) also burdened German-American relations, the U.S. Government adopted a wait and see policy when the payments stopped in 1932. The issue was laid to rest only in 1953 as a result of the London Debts Agreement, which includes the following loose clause:

"An examination of government claims against Germany arising from the first World War shall be deferred until there is an overall and final settlement of this matter."

Germany still nominally owes the United States about 1.5 billion dollars (occupation costs, mixed claims, etc.) stemming from World War I. But it is doubtful that payment will ever be demanded.

During the period of reparation politics, American policy on this question was also geared toward helping the German economy back on its feet. As early as 1922 Germany had once again become America's third best customer next to England and Canada. By 1925, American exports to Germany had risen to 1.8 billion Reich marks annually while German exports to the United States were barely 603 million marks. In a report he wrote on March 12, 1921, Undersecretary of State Norman Davis said:

"Through the highly industrial development of Europe prior to the war, Germany has become the axis, and the rehabilitation of Europe and its continued prosperity is most dependent on that of Germany."

Realizing this fact, the United States offered to conclude a friendship, trade and consular treaty with Germany giving it preferential treatment. This offer was made in 1923 at the height of the crisis touched off by the French occupation of the Ruhr area. The German Reichstag approved the treaty in 1925. Pre-war relations between German and American shipping companies were re-established soon after the war. The same was true for the electrical industries, where contatcs between Germany's AEG and America's General Electric were renewed. In fact, in a cooperation agreement concluded in 1922 and 1924, Siemens and Westinghouse divided the world markets among themselves.

Private American loans to German firms and municipalities did much to stimulate the German economy and transatlantic cooperation. Between 1924 and 1930, 135 separate American loans were made to cities such as Berlin, Cologne, Munich and Bremen and to companies including Krupp, Thyssen, AEG and Wintershall. Altogether 1.430 billion dollars flowed from the American to the German economy as the result of this assistance. This was in addition to 156 million dollars in short-term loans.

By 1930, no less then 79 American cooperations had either established their own subsidiaries or branches in Germany or had bought up German companies. American presence was particulary strong in the automobile branch: Ford, General Motors and Chrysler. Despite some German voices deploring this "foreign infiltration", even Adolf Hitler felt compelled to give his blessing to this type of support. In an interview with the "New York Evening Post" he said, "American capital investments in Germany will be safer under an National Socialist regime than under any other government."

The governments of the Weimar Republic took America's outstretched hand without hesitation. After all, trade cooperation between the two countries and American investments and loans could be used also as a political counterweight to Allied demands. America's interest in using Germany as a springboard to an "open door" trading policy in Europe coincided perfectly with Germany's hopes of getting back on its feet through cooperation with the United States. In addition, the Weimar governments wanted to base their foreign policy on close political ties to America. And Gustav Stresemann's policy of achieving reconciliation with France and Great Britain made this possible.

Foreign Minister Stresemann, who was awarded the Nobel Peace Prize in 1926, was able to gain admittance for Germany to the League of Nations. He was also mainly responsible for the conclusion of the Locarno-Pact, on respecting the German-French border and the demilitarization of the Rhineland as well as other agreements which promoted reconciliation with Germany's wartime adversaries. All of these steps were welcomed by the United States as contributing to a reduction of tensions in Europe and in keeping with American policy aimed at stabilizing the situation on the continent.

Friedrich Ebert, the first President of the Reich, gained America's respect by taking strong action against communist efforts to bring about a revolution in Germany and against the putsch plans of radicals on the right. This type of action prompted the American Embassy in Berlin to send the following report on German Social Democracy to Washington in 1922:

> "This party is no longer a group of agitators, but rather a party of intelligent liberal reform, peculiarly indispensable to the German Republic."

This recognition and support of moderate, democratic forces with a slight preference for the liberal-conservative element in German politics has been a traditional trait of American diplomacy, not only after the first but also following the second World War.

So, the period between 1918 and 1933 can be viewed as a time in which there was a rapid normalization of relations and increasing bilateral cooperation between Germany and the United States. Conclusion of the German-Soviet Rapallo-Treaty in 1922, however, cast a short shadow with far-reaching consequences on this transatlantic rapproachment.

In that treaty, the two weakened losers of the first World War reestablished diplomatic and trade relations and relinquished any demands the one may have had on the other. But this agreement produced the "Rapallo-complex"; a fear that the Soviet Union and Germany could unite against the West, and some Americans harbor this fear to this very day.

The German Reich signed the Kellog-Briand-Pact of August 27, 1928 with the greatest willingness. This treaty solemnly condemned the war but unfortunately provided no tools for enforcing peace. The agreement was the idea of Aristide Briand, the French Foreign Minister who together with Gustav Stresemann had made heroic efforts to reconcile France and Germany. U.S. Secretary of State Frank B. Kellog was also a father of the pact; in fact it was originally intended to be a bilateral agreement between France and the United States. But eventually it became a world peace treaty. It bears the signatures of sixty nations, but it turned out to have little more than symbolic significance.

The United States took a pronounced neutral position (thereby favoring Germany) on another provision of the Treaty of Versailles which the government of the Weimar Republic considered discriminatory and which the ultra right opposition was able to use for propaganda purposes. This was the clause calling for unilateral German disarmament. With a somewhat cautious eye on the ethnic German vote in America, President Herbert Hoover declared:

> "We are not a part of the Versailles Treaty and its limitations on German arms. That is solely a European question. The United

States has already declared that it takes no part in that discussion."

Germany at least did not have to anticipate American opposition to its efforts to win back its right to equality with the Western Powers in respect to armament.

Overall American policy toward Western Europe was somewhat ambivalent. The Locarno-Pact aroused some suspicion in Washington that Europe was in the process of building a "bloc". And at intervals, France indeed was operating in the direction of a "concentration" of the European nations to counter-balance American preponderance.

Stresemann, on the other hand, maneuvered against this French tactic designed to maintain the status quo in Europe. The German Foreign Minister wanted to keep open all options for revising the Treaty of Versailles.

Until 1932, a good relationship free of friction had developed between the United States and Germany. But then several things began to trouble Americans: the imminent collapse of the Weimar Republic; the overthrow of Heinrich Brüning as Chancellor of the Reich by an army-supported clique surrounding President of the Reich Paul von Hindenburg (who as a Field Marshal had commanded the German armies in the first World War), and alarming reports about the activities of the Nazis sent to the United States by American correspondents reporting from Germany.

Washington took a dim view of the appointment of Franz von Papen as Chancellor of the Reich at the head of an ultra-conservative minority government. As German Military Attaché in Washington during the first World War, von Papen (who was later to become Hitler's Vice-Chancellor) had participated in some sabotage plans, making a fool of himself by his dilettante behavior. The appointment of General Kurt von Schleicher (who was murdered by the Gestapo in June, 1934) as von Papen's successor didn't help to revive American trust in Germany. Commenting on von Papen's and Schleicher's demands that Germany be given an equal right to arm itself, Secretary of State Henry L. Stimson warned on September 15, 1932:

"If she (Germany) would behave well and regain that confidence, everybody would agree that she should have equality eventually and the Treaty (of Versailles) would be modified accordingly. But, unfortunately, she now by the present action, is taking the very step to forfeit that and none of us feel like relieving her from the obligation she has put herself under for a gradual process of disarmament."

And it was not long before America had even more reason to worry about Germany.

On January 30, 1933, President of the Reich von Hindenburg appointed "the simple Private who served in the first war" and "Fuehrer" of what had become the largest party in the German Reich (the NSDAP, National Socialist German Worker's Party) to be the new Chancellor of the Reich. Now the fate of the Germans had been placed in the hands of Adolf Hitler, the Austrian-born would-be painter who dreamed of establishing a "thousand-year Reich" to succeed Bismarck's German Empire.

This "Third Reich" had a life span of but twelve years, three months and ten days. But this was long enough for Germany to muster and deploy the greatest military power in its history. This power eventually was misused to conquer Europe from the Atlantic to the Volga, from the North Cape to the border of Egypt, and to drive Germany to ruin. Hitler made his place in history as one of the most destructive tyrants the world has ever known. And though the longevity of the "Third Reich" was relatively short, its brutality and nihilistic tyranny will be remembered for well beyond one thousand years.

Bringing about Hitler's demise and crushing his gigantic war machine was the work of many people; primarily the people of Great Britain and the Commonwealth and the people of the Soviet Union, who made the greatest sacrifices. But it almost certainly would not have been possible to achieve victory over the "Third Reich" without the help of President Franklin Delano Roosevelt and the United States. By supplying Germany's other adversaries with war material and food, by helping to win the decisive military battles in the air and by fielding the invasions of North Africa, Italy and France, America prevented Hitler from subjecting all of Europe (and his own people) to the bloodthirsty tyranny of his dictatorship for an unlimited span of time.

Indeed, aside from the conflict between the United States and Japan in the Pacific theater and the gigantic battles between Russian and German troops in Eastern Europe, the second World War was a German-American conflict in its decisive phases. This was not a battle for power or territory in the classic sense of war; it had the same dimension as religious wars in which completely different political systems and human delusions clashed on the battlefield. And it was fought by Germans and Americans who had much in common and no claims against each other which would have necessarily had to force them at each other's throats. While this is not the place to sketch biographies of Franklin D. Roosevelt and Adolf Hitler or to summarize the history of World War II, it is, however, necessary to cast a glance at the two men's personalities and some of the military highlights of the war. The diametrical contrast between these two men is, so to speak, the reflex of German-American antagonism for which there is no reason that can

Adolf Hitler, the "Fuehrer and Chancellor" of the short-lived Third Reich, is greeted at a rally by his chief propagandist, Joseph Goebbels, with Nazi salute. Martin Bormann (left of Hitler), the "evil spirit" of the chancellery, and Heinrich Himmler (right of Hitler), chief of the dreadful secret state police (Gestapo) and the SS or "elite guard" of the Nazi movement

be found in history. In his last days in the Reich-Chancellery in Berlin, Hitler belatedly came to realize his fatal mistake. As he phrased it, "The war with America is a tragedy; senseless and void of any reality." What he forgot to add was that he had provoked this tragedy himself.

Adolf Hitler came from simple surroundings and was only half-educated. He had a quick, perceptive mind, but he used this faculty for grasping things only superficially. He was driven by fanaticism and a strong will coupled with great oratorical talent. As a thorough egocentric, he relied exclusively on his own judgment. His political ideas sounded unreal and even absurd, but he was able to push them through to the point of self-annihilation. As a political tactician, he was a master at confusing and crippling his opponents. And he fascinated his collaborators with his seeming credibility and persuasive powers.

But Hitler made no secret of his intentions: as maniacal and demoniacal as his ideas seemed to onlookers, he was always soon to demonstrate that he meant them quite seriously. He despised democratic equality and preached the doctrine of the authoritarian Fuehrerstate. Intellectuals disgusted him and he vowed to do away with them along with the Marxists, Jews and Freemasons. He proclaimed the superiority of the "elite" (in this case Germanity) as a people destined to rule others and to whom the "inferior peoples" (above all the Slavs) owed subservience. The "elite", he preached, had a duty to exterminate all "brutes" and "subhumans". And he went about carrying out these policies with his hoards of "elite" uniformed murderers.

Hitler often spoke of peace because, he said, as a simple soldier he had "experienced the horrors of war". But at the same time he made preparations to wage the most terrible war of conquest the world has ever experienced. He promised the Germans that he would enlarge their cramped "Lebensraum" (living space) and went about making a nation of warriors out of them. He viewed faith and trust in dealings between nations as nothing more than deceit or outright premeditated fraud. And when democratic statesmen swore to these principles, he labled them cowards and weaklings. As far as economic policy was concerned, he believed in self-sufficiency. Militarily he thought only in terms of the European Continent; the oceans were completely alien to him.

On March 4, 1933, several weeks after Hitler's rise to power, Franklin D. Roosevelt was sworn in for the first time as President of the United States. Roosevelt, whose origins were in the East Coast Establishment, was a man-of-the-world. He had studied law at the country's best universities and had practiced it with great success in the State of New York. He had a personality which charmed others and had helped him to a long career in politics and government. He saw his life task as a liberal Democrat in gaining social security for the commonplace man and therefore introduced the "New Deal" as a means for overcoming the grave economic crisis in America.

For Franklin Roosevelt, the American traditions and principles of democracy and freedom were personal convictions for which he was prepared to fight. He knew how to appeal to people's idealism. But, on the other hand, he was a cool realist with a pronounced and masterful talent for manipulating public opinion to gain the support every President needs in order to be able to govern. In reality, however, he was much more intent on convincing or outwitting people than forcing his will on them by virtue of the authority of his office. He was not doctrinaire but rather an immensely practical man. His unusually strong will made it possible for him to go on to great achievements despite the handicap of partial paralysis which an attack of polio had left behind.

Roosevelt had grown up in secure economic surroundings. But when he moved into the White House, America was in the midst of the worst economic depression in its history and the world was facing its severest test of viability. As Assistant Secretary of the Navy during World War I, Roosevelt had been clearly on the side of the Western Allies and had been in favor of the Entente Powers and America dictating the terms of peace to Germany.

Hitler and Roosevelt were completely unknown factors to each other when they assumed office. In the summer of 1933, the American President said he had taken notice of one of Hitler's speeches in favor of peace "with enthusiasm". At approximately the same time, the German dictator said the following about Roosevelt: "I have a certain amount of liking for the President because he marches straight to his objective over Congress, over lobbies, over stubborn bureaucracies." Both men were fully engaged —each in his own way— with trying to lower unemployment and getting the economies moving again in their countries. Hitler immediately went about this by leaving the League of Nations and working toward quick rearmament. America hardly took notice of this; the United States was completely engrossed in its own problems. Washington was uneasy about Japan's actions against China and Manchuria (which undermined America's "open door policy") and believed they cast a bad omen of things to come. But America did not really understand what was going on in Germany.

Nevertheless, educated and intellectually-alert Americans were repelled by Hitler's treatment of the Jews, his ruthless elimination of all opposition through the construction of more and more concentration camps, and the terror of his secret police (Gestapo). Some prominent Americans (among them aviation hero Charles Lindbergh) actually expressed public admiration for the "disciplined reawakening of a people under authoritarian leadership". And the arrivals of German zeppelins, the boxing matches between Max Schmeling and Joe Louis and the colorful Olympic Games in Berlin in 1936 prompted many Americans to overlook what was really going on behind this brown curtain.

Roosevelt's mistrust of Nazi Germany was aroused much earlier than that of most of his countrymen. Hitler's speedy occupation of the demilitarized Rhineland, Germany's rush to rearm, the Nazi threats against European democracies and Germany's intervention in the

Max Schmeling, the "black hussar" from Germany, won and lost world heavy-weight boxing title in fights with American champion Joe Louis

Spanish Civil War were loud and clear messages of what the world could expect from Germany. And for Roosevelt personally, these were clear indications of Hitler's intention to spread out in Europe.

The American President was fully aware that the German dictator was not only pursuing military goals which here and there might give the impression of correcting some of the unjust consequences of the Treaty of Versailles. Roosevelt saw through Hitler's inhumanity and maniacal obsession with conquering the world with the help of Mussolini's Italy and the Emperor of Japan. And this is why Roosevelt reacted sooner and with more determination to the Fuehrer's provocations than other Western statesmen. In one of his most famous speeches, the Chicago "Quarantine Speech" of October 5, 1937, the President said:

> *"The political situation in the world ... is such as to cause grave concern and anxiety to all the peoples and nations who wish to live in peace and amity with their neighbors ... The present reign of terror and international lawlessness began a few years ago ... The landmarks and traditions which have marked the progress of*

civilization ... are being wiped away ... Innocent peoples,
innocent nations, are being cruelly sacrificed to a greed for power
and supremacy which is devoid of all sense of justice and human
considerations ... The peace-loving nations must make a con-
certed effort in opposition to those violations of treaties and those
ignorings of humane instincts which today are creating a state of
international anarchy and instability from which there is no escape
through mere isolation or neutrality ...
When an epidemic of physical disease starts to spread, the
community approves and joins in a q u a r a n t i n e of the
patients in order to protect the health of the community against
the spread of the disease.''

Hitler simply disregarded such warnings. His conception of America
was as uninformed, uneducated and confused as it was of other
countries. And the people around Hitler fed him mostly information
which merely strengthened his misconceptions and prejudices or
which they knew he wanted to hear. Hitler's views of the United States
swayed according to his erratic inclinations. Sometimes he expressed
great respect for America's industrial and organizational abilities, only
to scoff a few minutes later at its military potential. On some occasions
he was partial to America's Anglo-Saxon population. But as soon as it
became evident that the President was against him, Hitler attacked
Roosevelt, the Jews, the banking establishment and the American
press as being degenerate, immoral and materialistic.

Hitler's answer to the President's message appealing for peace on
April 14, 1939 was typical of his attitude toward Roosevelt. In this
appeal directed at both the Chancellor of the Reich and Benito Mussolini, Roosevelt had demanded assurances that the armed forces of
Germany and Italy would not attack 31 independent states, which he
listed by name. Many of them had no common border with Germany
and lay far beyond its normal reach. In a speech to the Reichstag on
April 28, 1939, Hitler answered with his usual mixture of sarcasm,
arrogance and distortions of history:

"President Roosevelt! I easily understand how the size of your
empire and the innerwealth of your country allow you to feel re-
sponsible for the destiny of the world and all of its peoples. I,
President Roosevelt, am in a much more modest and smaller
position. I can hardly feel responsible for the fate of the world
since that world showed no sympathy for the wretched fate of my
own people. I consider myself called upon by Providence to serve
only my people and to redeem them from their terrible suffering ...
I have overcome the chaos in Germany ... have increased pro-
duction enormously ... have been able to get all of seven million

unemployed back to productive work ... I have also tried to do away with that treaty (of Versailles), whose 448 articles constitute a vile rape, page-by-page. I have returned the stolen provinces to the Reich ... have restored the historic thousand-year unity of German lebensraum ... I have done this by my own strength as someone who only 21 years ago was an unknown laborer and soldier of my people ... You, Mr. President, are far better off. You are at the head of one of the largest and richest countries in the world and therefore have the time and leisure ... to concern yourself with universal problems."

This speech was hardly less than a torch of war. Hitler simply ignored America's determination not to tolerate all that the German Fuehrer had in store for the world.

What probably encouraged Hitler to ignore the handwriting on the wall was the fact that between 1938 and 1940, he had been able to score victories over West European democracies without the United States taking direct action. There were numerous developments which confirmed Roosevelt's worst fears and prophecies: the Anschluß (annexation) of Austria, which had twice been prevented by France and Italy from voluntarily joining the German Reich after 1918; the Munich Agreement on the transfer of the Sudeten Territories to Germany and the annexation of Czechoslovakia which soon followed, and the non-aggression pact with Stalin; Germany's quick victory over France and its simultaneous occupation of Norway, Denmark, Holland, Belgium and Luxembourg; and England's retreat from Dunkirk.

Roosevelt issued several personal appeals to Hitler in an effort to prevent the worst, but he avoided making any direct American commitment. The moment for that came when the air battle over Britain and the "Atlantic battle" of submarine warfare threatened to destroy the last remaining pillar of democracy off the coast of Europe. Prime Minister Winston Churchill was the congenial partner with whom the American President could work together to overpower Germany's Hitler and other totalitarian regimes. Roosevelt fully agreed with Churchill's remark that "Germany, the rabid dog of Europe, has broken its chain again."

Since until the Japanese attack on Pearl Harbor a large majority of Americans had been in favor of supporting Great Britain but against active American participation in the war against the Third Reich, Roosevelt had to conduct a policy short of war and stressing nonbelligerence. He carried this out in masterful fashion which brought much American weight to bear without the United States laying a hand on Germany directly. These activities included loosening the neutrality laws by the immediate delivery of weapons to Great Britain; turning

President Franklin D. Roosevelt and Prime Minister Winston Churchill on deck of the "Prince of Wales" after shaping the Atlantic Charter

over fifty destroyers in return for eight naval bases in an area extending from Newfoundland to the Caribbean, and expanding the American neutrality zone to cover more of the mid-Atlantic, with U.S. Navy ships patrolling the area.

Following Hitler's attack on the Soviet Union on June 22, 1941, the lend-lease-law was also applied to support the Russians. The political culmination of this campaign of offensive support for the Western democracies was the signing of the "Atlantic-Charter" aboard the American cruiser "Augusta" on August 14, 1941. This charter set the guidelines for establishing a new world political order following the war; these principles were not to be applied to Germany.

Once again, just as a quarter of a century before, it inevitably came to German-American clashes on the Atlantic. An incident on the high seas prompted President Roosevelt (on September 11, 1941) to order the U.S. Navy to "shoot on sight" any German warship they should encounter: a German U-boat had fired on (but missed) the American destroyer "Greer" because it had radioed the position of the submarine to the British. In this way, the President had been able to make the United States de facto into a co-belligerent of Great Britain against Germany.

But Hitler wanted to postpone the war America until his expected victory over Russia. On June 21, 1941, he gave the following order: "The Fuehrer wants all clashes with the United States to be avoided until there is clarity in how 'Operation Barbarossa' develops; that is, for several weeks." And all the way up to October, 1941, Hitler rejected requests from the High Command of the German Navy for permission to take stronger action against the Americans. In fact, just three weeks before Pearl Harbor he again insisted that his ships exercise restraint in dealing with the U.S. Navy. He was satisfied with looking on as the Americans were put under pressure in the Far East by the Japanese, Germany's other ally in the triangular pact with Italy which was intended to neutralize the United States.

Germany and Japan, however, never really brought their military policies and strategies into line with each other; there was no coordination of military action. Hitler, for example, attacked the Soviet Union without giving advance notice to Tokyo and the Japanese attack on Pearl Harbor came as a complete surprise to Berlin. But for Hitler the news was tantamount to deliverance from a state of suspension in which he had placed Germany's behavior toward America. Four days after Pearl Harbor, Germany declared war on the United States. Hitler obviously did not realize that this act had sealed the fate and numbered the days of his beloved "Thousand-year Reich".

The United States now set its enormous resources and energies into high gear. After stabilizing the situation in the Pacific, the United States gave the European theater of operations top priority. In 1942, the Americans landed in North Africa and (following the capitulation of Germany's troops in Tunisia in 1943) also in southern Italy and Sicily. While the British bombed German cities and industries by night, the Americans concentrated on their targets by daylight. But despite this hail of destruction, Germany's armaments production reached its peak in 1944. It was not until the United States started to concentrate on destroying Germany's essential nerve centers (its transportation facilities and plants producing synthetic gasoline) that America was able to really neutralize the German war effort.

Hitler's armies had been weakened decisively by Soviet offensives and the capitulation at Stalingrad on January 31, 1943. One week earlier, at the Conference of Casablanca on January 24, 1943, Roosevelt had announced his terms for ending this second world conflict:

"The elimination of German, Japanese and Italian war power

means the u n c o n d i t i o n a l surrender by Germany, Italy and Japan. That means a reasonable assurance of future world peace. It does not mean the destruction of the population of Germany, Italy or Japan, but it does mean the destruction of the philosophy in those countries which are based on conquest and the subjugation of other people."

This demand for "unconditional surrender" was Roosevelt's answer to the "total war" which Hitler had declared on the world.

On June 6, 1944, America led the Allies in the successful Normandy Invasion. The allied thrust continued through France to the German industrial areas with only a temporary setback in "The Battle of the Bulge", Germany's last major offensive. They rolled back Germany's western front while the victorious Russians marched into Berlin. The largest military struggle in history ended with Germany's unconditional surrender in Reims on May 7, 1945, a ceremony which was repeated the following day in the East Berlin suburb of Karlshorst for the benefit of Russia's marshals.

But the man who dedicated all of his personal strength and America's greatest efforts to the struggles on the Pacific and the Atlantic-European fronts did not live to see the final victory. Franklin D. Roosevelt had died on April 12, 1945. The opponent whom he had demolished to prevent German predominance in Europe and to put an end to uninhibited expansion of a brutal dictatorship outlived him by only eighteen days: Adolf Hitler committed suicide in the bunker of the Reich-Chancellery on April 30, 1945.

In the final years of his life, Roosevelt had worked together with Churchill and Stalin on post-war arrangements; primarily on what was to be done with Germany. The three leaders conferred at the Teheran-Conference of November 1943, and again at the Yalta-Conference on the Crimea in February, 1945. The final meeting of the three Allies (with President Harry S. Truman representing the United States) was held in Potsdam in late July, 1945. They agreed on five basic measures to be taken after the war: the complete demilitarization of Germany, punishment of its war criminals, eradication of all traces of National Socialism, a democratization of Germany and the relinquishment of sizeable parts of Germany's pre-war territory to the Soviet Union and Poland. The latter measure was originally intended to be provisional.

The war had been an unprecedented bloodbath which took approximately fifty million lives, about sixteen million had been soldiers, of which more than six million were Soviet, 3.5 million German and 320,000 American (in both the Far East and Europe). The total material cost of the war had been 1,500 billion dollars, including 230 billion in destroyed property. In a world of shambles and suffering, only America was intact.

Roosevelt's successor, President Truman, had to deal with disastrous conditions in Europe: cities, industries and transportation facilities had been demolished; millions of foreigners who had been subjected to forced labor in Germany and German refugees who had been expelled from the German territories transferred to Poland and the Soviet Union or those re-incorporated into Czechoslovakia flooded the devastated country; food, clothing, shelter, heating fuel and other essentials were scarce; and all civilian administrations had ceased to function in Central Europe.

It is hard to imagine what would have become of the Germans if the United States had not decided to extend a helping hand. America did this following only a very short interval of hesitation during which there were thoughts of revenge, of transfoming Germany into an agricultural state and of forcing it into an unlimited period of subservience. Indeed, America's quick decision to help rebuild Germany after 1945 rather than render it completely ineffective was dictated by reason and foresight. For Europe can hardly exist without a productive Germany and it seemed advisable to include Germany as quickly as possible in a security system. This was becoming all the more necessary in view of the East-West confrontation which was already beginning to take shape.

The generosity which America demonstrated (quickly and without quibbling) in helping the Western part of Germany to recover from the war was simply incredible. In contrast to 1918, this time the United States assumed political leadership in reorganizing conditions in Western Europe. And in their dealings with Germany, the Americans acted with self-confidence derived from superior strength.

The immediate post-war period, however, was still marked by the disdain, disgust and outright hate which many Americans felt as the full horror of Hitlers's twelve-year reign was uncovered: almost six million Jews had been murdered in concentration and death camps or by SS commandoes operating behind the front in Russia; the Germans had decimated Polands political, economic, academic and cultural leadership: they had permitted millions of Soviet prisoners of war to starve to death; millions of foreigners had been carried off to perform slave labor in Germany; and the Nazis had committed atrocities against their own opposition at home. These revelations prompted initial American occupation policy to be geared toward punishment and re-education; both were experiments with good intentions but of dubious success.

The policy of punishment and re-education had two goals: punishment of war crimes and denazification. Following the first world war, passing judgement on war criminals had been left up to German courts. They handed down few and minimal sentences. But in 1945, the victorious Allies (the United States, Britain, France and the Soviet Union) took this into their own hands and on the basis of the Four Power Agreements concluded in London created a military tribunal in Nuremberg to conduct the trials.

In this process of justice, two protected interests faced each other in an insoluble conflict: on the one hand, the gruesome deeds of the leaders of the Third Reich virtually cried out for punishment and atonement. But on the other hand, it was of utmost importance to demonstrate to the German people the principle of rule of law. Acting on American initiative in this dilemma, the Allies created completely new principles of criminal law and unprecedented procedural rules for applying them. The crimes of preparing and waging a war of aggression and crimes against humanity were added to the list of what had been classified and treated as "crimes" up to then.

Not only individuals but entire organizations were indicted. These international laws were also applied retroactively in violation of the principle of "nulla poena sine lege". The judges and prosecutors were citizens of the victorious powers; the defendants and their lawyers were citizens of the defeated nation. This violated the principle that there should be no conflicts of interest between those who pass judgement and those who are judged. But the most serious flaw in the Nuremberg procedure became evident much later; namely when it turned out that the newly-adopted principles of international law were not recognized as binding by any country in the world and were not applied anywhere else, even though innumerous war crimes have been committed since 1945.

Sentences were handed down in the Nuremberg War Crimes Trials against 23 leading Nazi functionaries, politicians and officers of the Third Reich. Twelve persons were sentenced to death, ten of whom were hanged. Luftwaffe Chief Marshal Hermann Göring escaped the gallows by poisoning himself in his cell. The leader of the Nazi labor movement, Robert Ley, also committed suicide. Martin Bormann, Hitler's Administrator of the Reich and right-hand man, was sentenced to death in absentia. Three defendants were acquitted, the rest were sentenced to life imprisonment or long term confinement.

The last relic of this trial against Germany's major war criminals turned out to be Rudolf Hess, Hitler's former deputy, who at this writing (1976) was the last prisoner in the huge Spandau Prison in Berlin. There, he is guarded by dozens of soldiers from the Four Power nations. In 1941, the "Deputy of the Führer" (as was Hess'

The end at Nuremberg:
Hitler's surviving chieftains face trial at Four Power court

official title) had taken it upon himself to fly to Scotland to try to promote peace with England without Hitler's knowledge. Rudolf Hess, believed to be only partially sane, has been in prison ever since.

Several hundred more war criminals were sentenced in the American Zone of Occupation, among them buisnessmen, doctors, policemen, judges, lawyers and others wo had committed crimes against humanity during the Third Reich. About 400 death sentences were handed down, of which 250 were carried out. Similar trials were held in the other three occupation zones, for which approximately 5,000 persons were extradited from the American Zone. The most drastic event in the course of these trials was the execution of 49 former guards at the Mauthausen concentration camp.

America's main contribution to the democratization of Western Germany therefore was not so much the war crimes trials and the denazification. Of much greater importance to this process were the creation of Germany's self-administering authorities, the consolidation of the three western zones of occupation into the Federal Republic of Germany established on a democratic Basic Law, the reintroduction of freedom of the press and a free economy based on competition and supply and demand.

America's purpose in doing this was to revitalize the middle-class structure of German society and to immunize its basically conservative character against movements from the extreme right (neonazism) and from the extreme left (communism). And the policies pursued initially by the American occupation authorities as well as America's alliance policies in and with West Germany ever since have been highly successful in achieving those goals.

The most significant milestones of American postwar policy on Germany are as follows:

1) Early abandonment of the Joint Chiefs of Staff directive (No. 1067) calling for harsh treatment of Germans and strictly prohibiting fraternization.

2) Inclusion of the American, French and British Zones of Occupation in GARIOA (Government Appropriations for Relief in Occupied Areas), under which right after the end of the war 1.8 billion dollars' worth of food, medicine and fertilizer were delivered to the Western part of Germany.

3) Large amounts of private aid in the form of "CARE packages" containing essentials.

4) Inclusion of Western Germany in the plan for European reconstruction (Marshall Plan) of April 3, 1948, which was later called the European Recovery Program (ERP). Of the approximately 13 billion dollars which were appropriated for overall European recovery, Germany received 1.282 billion. The Mutual Security Act of October 10, 1951 gave Germany another 253 million and loans amounting to about 17 million dollars. This means that Germany's "economic miracle" was sparked by more than 1.55 billion dollars in American assistance. And added to what was granted earlier as part of GARIOA, American economic assistance to postwar Germany amounted to 3.5 billion dollars.

5) Slowing down the dismantling of German industry and then the early combining of the three western occupation zones, primarily as the result of American initiative. Following the currency reform of 1948, and ratification of a Federal Constitution (which had been worked out by a German "Parliamentary Council") by the West German states, the "Bundesrepublik Deutschland" (The Federal Republic of Germany) was born

111

on May 23, 1949. Its territory is what were once the French, British and American Zones of Occupation.

6) The step-by-step transfer of full sovereignty to the Federal Republic through the Occupation Statute of September 21, 1949, the Petersberg Agreement of November 22, 1949, the official termination of the state of war by the Western Powers on July 9, 1951, and finally the signing of the Treaty on Germany on May 26, 1952. This transfer was completed on October 21, 1954, with the signing of the Paris Treaties and the lifting of the Occupation Statute on May 5, 1955, by the western Allied High Commissioners. With the exception of some reservations of the three western powers pertaining to Germany as a whole and Berlin, the Federal Republic of Germany now is completely sovereign.

7) Securing the viability of the three western sectors of Berlin following the Soviet blockade of land and waterway transit routes to the city by the creation of an Allied airlift, operated mainly by the United States Air Force. In 277,000 separate flights, the Americans and British kept the strangled city alive by supplying it with about 1.8 million tons of food, clothing, medicine, coal and other essentials. The Soviets gave up after eleven months and in May, 1949, ended their physical blockade of West Berlin.

8) Inclusion of the Federal Republic of Germany in the North Atlantic Treaty Organization (NATO) defense alliance on May 9, 1955. This followed rejection of a "European Defense Community" by the French National Assembly on August 30, 1954. West German membership in NATO marked the beginning of the re-armament of Western Germany. The Federal Republic now has an approximately 500,000 man-strong Army, Air Force and Navy. The United States delivered the first equipment for these forces.

The rebirth of the larger part of what had once been the German Empire in the form of the Federal Republic of Germany was the result of a joint policy on Germany on the part of the United States, Great Britain and France in cooperation with the leaders of all of West Germany's democratic political parties. But the imitator and driving force behind this rebirth undeniably was the United States.

Washington determined the speed and means with which the defeated enemy was brought back to life. The United States took the decisive steps leading toward West German inclusion in NATO, the Western defense alliance. American diplomacy countered all attempts to detach areas of land belonging to West Germany, though it ac-

Berlin airlift of 1948/49 overpowers Soviet blockade—and Berliners enthusiastically wave to Allied "raisin-bombers"

Humanitarian aid from America: Ernst Reuter, Mayor of Berlin (center), distributes the millionth Care parcel

cepted the temporary connection of the steel-producing Saar Territory to France. America opposed all attempts to prevent economic recovery in the three western zones and in the western sectors of Berlin. This was the case even though Washington's Directive No. 1067 to the Supreme Commander of U. S. Forces in Europe, General Dwight D. Eisenhower, had read:

> *"You are to take absolutely no steps with an eye toward the ecnomic reconstruction of Germany or intended to maintain or strengthen the German economy."*

The plan proposed by President Roosevelt's Secretary of the Treasury Henry Morgenthau Jr. to transform Germany into an agricultural state without heavy industry and with a standard of living not to surpass that of other European states was also quickly dropped. And wiser from its bad experiences following the first World War, this time American diplomacy opposed any German reparations in the form of cash payments in hard currency. The Allies discussed reparations amounting of twenty billion dollars, of which the Soviet Union was to get ten billion. In the early stages of the discussions, the United States government went along with the reparation plans calling for dismantling and transferring industrial equipment, tapping German production and using German prisoners of war for labor. The Americans had little influence on whether these measures were carried out in the British and French Zones and none at all on what went on in the Soviet Zone. But (in contrast to the other three victorious powers) the United States did not remove any goods from its area of occupation for its own use. On the contrary, the Americans were instrumental in having the number of 1,800 German industrial plants originally slated to be dismantled (in the Potsdam Agreement of 1945) reduced to 680 in the Petersberg Agreement concluded at the end of 1949.

But the United States did not give up its claim to German compensation altogether. German assets in America amounting to about 500 million dollars was confiscated. A fraction of this was later returned to individuals in amounts of up to ten thousand dollars each. American companies benefited immensely from the confiscation and release for use (by all victors of World War II) of 150,000 domestic and 200,000 foreign German patents. Thus, the Germans were forced to make "reparations in the form of intellectual and technical property" totaling an amount which would almost be impossible to calcuate. And finally, the Germans had to carry heavy burdens of the American and other countries' occupation costs.

An indication that at least America was going to make the transition to a rational policy so vital to the recovery of Western Germany was contained in an address given by Secretary of State James F. Byrnes

114

in Stuttgart on September 6, 1946. First he pointed out that the United States intended to fulfill the commitments it had made pertaining to Germany in the Potsdam Agreement. Then he lamented that realization of the agreement's provisions concerning the economic unity of Germany and the development of its democratic institutions had been obstructed by the actions of other members of the Four Power Administration. And he left no doubt that he was referring to the Soviet Union and France.

"The American people," Byrnes continued, "want peace. They have long since ceased to talk of a hard or of a soft peace for Germany. This never has been the real issue. What we want is a lasting peace." Byrnes then went on to list what would be the goals of American occupation policy from that moment on:

"Freedom from militarism will give the German people the opportunity to apply their great energies and abilities to the works of peace ... and in time, to take an honorable place among the members of the United Nations.

There should be changes in the levels of industry agreed upon by the Allied Control Commission if Germany is not to be administered as an economic unit as the Potsdam Agreement requires. Reparations from current production would be wholly incompatible with the levels of industry now established under the Potsdam Agreement.

The United Staates is firmly of the belief that Germany should be administered as an economic unit ...

The American government is unwilling to accept responsibility for the needless aggravation of economic distress that is caused by the failure of the Allied Control Council to give the German people a chance to solve some of their most urgent economic problems.

A common financial policy is essential for the successful rehabilitation of Germany. A program of drastic fiscal reform to place Germany on a sound financial basis is urgently required.

It never was the intention of the American government to deny to the German people the right to manage their own internal affairs as soon as they were able to do so in a democratic way.

The purpose of the occupation did not contemplate a prolonged foreign dictatorship of Germany's peacetime economy or a prolonged foreign dictatorship of Germany's internal political life. The Potsdam agreement did not provide that there should never be a central German government.

It is the view of the American government that the German people throughout Germany, under proper safeguards, should now be given the primary responsibility for the running of their own affairs.

The American people want to help the German people to win their way back to an honorable place among the free and peaceloving nations of the world." (excerpts.)

There were many Americans serving their country in Germany who were as much the architects of this policy of reconciliation as were their Presidents and Secretaries of State. General Lucius D. Clay, who first was Eisenhower's deputy and then the Military Governor in the United States Zone from 1947 to 1949, was very popular in Germany. He was especially active in organizing the economic and political consolidation of the three Western zones, the German currency reform and the Berlin airlift. Colonel Howley was equally popular in Berlin. There, as American Commandant, he had kept watch during the blockade like a fearless warrior.

During Germany's transition to self-administration and to being incorporated into the Western community of nations, the country's political leaders depended greatly on the advice and help of three American High Commissioners: John J. McCloy (1949—1952), Walter J. Donnelly (1952—1953), and James B. Conant (1953—1955). They worked well with such congenial German partners as Berlin Lord Mayor Ernst Reuter, an energetic anti-communist Social Democrat; Federal Economics Minister Ludwig Erhard, the "Father of the German Economic Miracle", who instituted a liberal economic system with social safeguards; and Erhard's fellow Christian Democrat, Chancellor Konrad Adenauer. He was probably the West German politican of the immediate post-war period best known to Americans.

Adenauer was as convinced as his American partners that the post-war policies of those parts of Germany not occupied by the Soviets would have to be closely aligned with those of the Western Powers, especially the United States. And he was also convinced that German-French conciliation had to be another pillar of German post-war policy. In pursuing these policies, Adenauer worked together closely with Secretary of State John Foster Dulles as well as with France; first with Foreign Minister Robert Schuman and later with President Charles de Gaulle. West Germany's first Chancellor was in complete agreement with Dulles that the spread of communism had to be halted at the door of Central Europe.

Dr. Adenauer shared Minister Schuman's and President de Gaulle's belief that the free part of Western Europe should assume an increasingly independent role in world politics in conjunction with the United States. But as the years went by, these principles not always coincided with the development of relations between the United States and the Soviet Union on the one hand and relations between Washington and Paris on the other.

Adenauer, the extremely self-confident "grand old man" of the Federal Republic, was able to negotiate almost complete sovereignty for West Germany in exchange for a German contribution to Western defense. On this basis and in conjunction with America's policy of containment (and for a while also with Dulles' roll-back philosophy), he had hoped to be able to build up a joint position of strength with the Western Powers. And Adenauer hoped that from this position of strength it would be possible to negotiate a peaceful relationship of a reunified Germany with the Soviet Union.

Together with France and the other members of the original Common Market (Italy, Belgium, Holland and Luxembourg) Adenauer wanted to create a supranational community, a United Europe. At times, Konrad Adenauer was able to make progress in this direction. But the two main goals—German reunification and the political integration of Europe—have still not been achieved and appear to be far-off.

Today, historians ponder that perhaps German-American cooperation (resulting from the need for providing West Germany with economic stability and tying it to the West) developed too quickly and did not give enough consideration and maybe not even enough thought to the interests of the Soviet Union. Until the middle of the 1950's, the Soviet Union had demonstrated some interest in the creation of a reunified Germany. To be sure, Moscow placed two conditions on this: that the Soviet Union would then have to be put in a position to exert considerable influence on the development of all of Germany, and that this unified Germany not be allowed to link up either politically or militarily with the West. In the cold war era, it was not possible to bring American and Soviet policies on Germany into agreement with each other. The aphorism once expressed by a West European diplomat was accepted by both sides: "Full control of half of Germany is better than only half control of all of Germany."

As the Dulles-Adenauer era began to come to an end, these two statesmen had started cautious deliberations an how the Federal Republic of Germany might be able to achieve a modus vivendi with the Soviet Union on the basis of the status quo, which, of course, was only to be of a temporary nature. The foundation for their joint reunification policy under international law had been laid in Article 7 of the Treaty on Relations Between the Federal Republic of Germany and the Three Western Powers concluded on May 26, 1952 and of March 30, 1955 respectively:

> *"The undersigned countries are agreed that an essential goal of*

their joint policies is the achievement of a peace settlement for Germany as a whole, freely-negotiated between Germany and its former adversaries, which should form the foundation for a lasting peace. Furthermore they are agreed that the final regulation of Germany's borders must be deferred until such a settlement.

Until the conclusion of a peace settlement, the undersigned countries will work together to achieve their joint goal with peaceful means; a reunified Germany with a free, democratic constitution similar to that of the Federal Republic and which is integrated in the European community.

The three powers shall consult the Federal Republic on all matters pertaining to the exercising of their rights which affect Germany as a whole."

A comparison of this text with present-day realities shows clearly what changes have taken place in the meantime. There is no peace settlement for Germany, but a de-facto state of peace exists between the Four Powers (United States, Soviet Union, Britain, France) as well as with the Federal Republic of Germany and the German Democratic Republic. Germany's borders in the East and West as well as the border dividing the two German states have been recognized in fact if not in law, accepted, even though there still is no peace treaty. And there is little talk of reunification, a democratic constitution for all of Germany or the integration of a unified Germany in the European Community. So, the general treaty between the three Western Powers and the Federal Republic (1952/55 and still in effect) today does not signify much more than an intention expressed at that time regarding their policy on Germany. This intention has been underlined on many occasions up to now, but it is difficult to imagine how it can be transformed into reality.

The lack of progress of the policy designed to bring about German reunification can be attributed mainly to East-West antagonism in Europe. In addition to the Soviet Union's refusal to accept the West's concrete conditions for reuniting the two parts of Germany, strong resistance to this idea on the part of France and West Germany's smaller neighbors as well as Britain's hesitancy to move in this direction have also played a substantial role in keeping this question in the background.

Even the intention of having West Germany become a member of NATO was not limited to wanting to have the Germans make a military contribution to the Alliance. When in the course of the East-West conflict it became inevitable for the Germans to rearm, the West German military forces were absorbed into the defense organization. And

118

when Stalin—shortly before his death—proposed that Germany be reunited as a completely neutral country with a national army made up of fifteen divisions, the governments of the United States and West Germany refused to even discuss the plan. They regarded it as a Soviet maneuver intended only to prevent the rearming of Western Germany within the framework of the Western Community.

As the main brace of Western policy on Germany, the United States would probably have been the only one of the victorious powers to go along with German reunification without reservation, provided that this new Germany would be able to develop freely into a democracy and not be put under the influence of the Soviet Union and its allies. This was why of all of the Western Allies, the United States was most persevering in supporting the position of Chancellor Konrad Adenauer's five cabinets (between 1949 and 1963) that Germany must be reunited as the outcome of free elections. They moved away from this policy only after it became absolutely certain that Moscow would not go along with this under any circumstances because free elections would have meant the end of the communist regime in the German Democratic Republic and the absorption of this artificial state in a united, democratic Germany.

The "ugly wall" in Berlin, constructed by East Germany's communist government on August 13th, 1961—a brutal symbol of division

President John F. Kennedy, visiting Berlin on June 26th, 1963, with mayor Willy Brandt (center) and Chancellor Konrad Adenauer (right)—a postwar climax of German-American interdependence

American policy toward the Soviet Union changed following the election of President John F. Kennedy in 1960. The new goals of accomodation and detente logically prompted Germany's "Ostpolitik" to move in the direction of "recognizing the realities which had come to be since World War II" (a longstanding demand from Moscow). Part of those "facts of life" are the division of Germany and Europe and western tolerance of the Soviet sphere of influence in Central and Eastern Europe.

The period of transition between 1959 and 1966 saw the first major frictions between the Federal Republic and the United States. These have been played down in public for the sake of unity within the Alliance. They came about because Adenauer tried to get the United States to bring German reunification through free elections into direct connection with disarmanent negotiations and other bilateral talks between Washington and Moscow. Adenauer wanted reunification to be made a precondition for any developments in Europe in which the Soviets were interested.

But President Kennedy began to feel that this particular political tie to America's German Ally was inhibiting his own freedom of movement. The policies pursued by General de Gaulle, who gradually began to withdraw France from NATO military integration (a process he completed in 1966) and developed an independent nuclear force under French control, made the situation even more difficult for both Bonn and Washington. The Federal Republic of Germany found itself in the midst of the contrast between the "Atlanticists" and the "Gaullists". In January of 1963, Konrad Adenauer concluded the French-German Treaty of Friendship and Coorperation, which included some military clauses. This awakened the mistrust of the Kennedy Administration, which became evident despite a smiling outward appearance. Indeed, there were several points of intensive friction between the young President and Bonn's "grand old man".

But the simmering has never progressed to flames. This was mainly because Adenauer had a much stronger Atlantic than Gaullist soul. And in the case of the first Chancellor's successors (Ludwig Erhard, 1963—1966; Kurt Georg Kiesinger, 1966—1969; Willy Brandt, 1969—1974, and then Chancellor Helmut Schmidt), they much more consciously tended toward the United States or simply avoided getting involved in French-American controversies.

Some heavy but quite bearable burdens were put on German-American diplomatic relations following Adenauer's resignation. What brought on the friction was the controversial Soviet-American bilateral cooperation in the field of nuclear restraint and the fact that German problems were not given enough consideration in some agreements, Bonn believed. The Christian-Democratic cabinets in Bonn complained that German interests had not received enough consideration in such agreements as the one on partial renunciation of atomic testing and that on non-proliferation. Some circles in Bonn felt that these agreements had relegated the Federal Republic to an inferior military position. And every two years minor friction was caused by the renegotiation of German-American agreements on offsetting the currency drain on the U. S. Treasury by the presence in West Germany of approximately 200,000 American troops ("offset agreements").

America's use of West German territory for transferring American weapons from the arsenals of the Seventh U. S. Army to Israel during the Middle East War in October, 1973 without consulting the Bonn government caused a difficult situation. An official statement issued on October 25th, 1973 says that the Undersecretary of the West German

Foreign Ministry had informed U. S. Ambassador Martin Hillenbrand that

> "The Federal Republic of Germany's strict neutrality in the Middle East conflict does not make it possible to permit weapons to be delivered from depots in the Federal Republic to one of the warring parties, making use of the Federal Republic or its facilities."

Nevertheless, none of these developments caused serious injury to German-American friendship. They were much the manifestation of the increasing self-confidence of the Germans also toward their principal ally and the occasional minor conflicts of interest with the Americans were easily settled.

Sometimes the two partners' bilateral relations were clouded by developments not directly connected with their dealings with each other. For example, in the course of Soviet-American rapproachment there was a short-lived uneasiness in Bonn that Washington might sell legitimate German interests down the river. But this was surely a misjudgement of the situation by German politicians not sufficiently versed in anlyzing the coherence of world politics. A few years later the misjudgement was on the other side: when Chancellor Willy Brandt set his policy of relaxing tensions with Eastern Europe in motion, some circles in the White House and State Department became uneasy that West Germany might be moving toward neutrality, to a status somewhat along the lines of Finland.

U.S. involvement in Indochina was another perceptible burden on American-German relations. The government of the Federal Republic of Germany often expressed solidarity with America's intentions, but there was vehement criticism from the West German population, primarily from the country's youth, academic circles and the left wing of the Social Democratic Party. The Bonn government eventually began to worry that the proportions and length of this commitment might cause the United States to neglect its interest in Europe. And indeed, Washington felt less and less inclined to promote Western European integration.

Presidents Kennedy and Johnson and Secretary of State Dean Rusk had repeatedly called on Western Europe to "speak with one voice", also to the United States. But instead, Washington witnessed a decline in efforts to achieve European political integration. In the sober view of the Americans, the Old Continent was behaving more and more like a European kindergarten. Around the middle of the 1960's, American diplomacy therefore made an almost undetectable but nevertheless significant change in its policy toward Europe. From then on, Washington no longer played the role of the great advocate of supranational

West European integration. The United States adopted a more reserved position and left the question of whether and in what form they want to cooperate more or less up to the Europeans.

All of these deviations and irritations affected German-American relations either directly or indirectly. Time and again Washington urged West Germany to take the lead in working toward European unity, to assume "greater political responsibility" and for it to stop being a political dwarf while an economic giant. But the United States never coupled these suggestions with advice on *how* Bonn could maintain the harmony it had laboriously achieved with its western neighbors, the Soviet Union and Eastern Europe (in the interest of international political stability) and at the same time play an even greater role on the stage of world politics.

Considering all of these aspects then, it is no wonder that between 1960 and 1970 there were some German-American tempests in a teacup. For example President Johnson's decision to drop the project of a Multilateral Nuclear Force (MLF) caused some disappointment in West Germany, which was to have been included in this project. But not enough other countries were willing to share the costs of a MLF. Then, political and industrial circles felt they had been placed at a disadvantage by the NATO committee which coordinates the exports of strategically important goods from the Alliance countries to the East Bloc, "COCOM", when—at the urging of the United States—it recommended that West Germany not sell large quantities of steel piping to the Soviet Union. Lyndon Johnson got Chancellor Ludwig Erhard into hot water and serious trouble by talking him into delivering American tanks belonging to the German Army to Israel. This had hardly leaked out when almost all Arab states broke diplomatic relations with West Germany. The relations remained severed for several years. Then U.S. Secretary of Defense Robert S. McNamara came up with a curious diplomatic request: he asked the Germans to at least send one unit of German army engineers to South Vietnam to help build roads and brigdes. When the German Ambassador in Washington, Heinrich Knappstein, immediately and in no uncertain terms refused, McNamara was taken aback.

Soviet-American understanding of nuclear armament and armament limitation (which has been continued in the form of the Strategic Arms Limitation Talks, SALT) no longer is a cause of friction between Washington and Bonn. There are enough other things to worry about. But there is a basic question raised by this which has yet to be answered. The Federal Republic of Germany long ago renounced possession of nuclear weapons and since has also ratified the Nuclear Non-Proliferation Treaty. But as far as national security is concerned, this puts West Germany in an inferior position. Next to the United States, West Germany has the largest amount of conventional military power in NATO. But it does not have any say in the deployment of nuclear weapons. The NATO Nuclear Planning Group (which was formed on American initiative and in which Germany, unlike other European non-nuclear members of NATO, has a permanent seat), is hardly, many observers feel, an adequate substitute for German nuclear co-determination within the framework of the joint Western institutions.

But none of these small or somewhat larger discrepancies have shaken the foundation of German-American cooperation. In fact, the causal and chronological concurrence of the new German policy toward Eastern Europe with the policy of relaxing tensions with the Soviet Union initiated by President Eisenhower and then pursued with great vigor by John F. Kennedy actually created but another platform of common German-American interests.

These developments, which still today determine the overall situation in Central Europe, were the result of two decisive developments which flowed together. The United States reacted with great determination to Khrushchev's "Berlin Ultimatum" in which he threatened that the Soviet Union would conclude a separate peace treaty with East Germany and give it control of the transit traffic routes to the divided city if West Berlin were not given the status of a "free city"; that is, if it did not sever all of its essential ties to the Federal Republic of Germany. President Kennedy immediately called up reserves and, when he met the Soviet party leader in Vienna, rejected Khrushchev's demands. But American reaction to the building of the ugly communist wall in Berlin in August, 1961, was mild. Washington took into account that by stopping the swelling stream of refugees leaving East Germany, the situation in the German Democratic Republic would become more stable. And this, in turn, could reduce tensions with the Soviets over Berlin.

The second decisive event was the Cuban missile crisis. Kennedy's demonstration of determination caused Moscow to realize that clear demarcation of spheres of interest with the United States would be more advisable than confrontation. Both super powers now recognized the need for avoiding nuclear war. Berlin and Cuba were what in essence triggered the policy of detente. West Germany's "Ostpolitik" is a complementary element of this policy, and not an independent factor. But it includes specific *German* components.

West Germany's policy of normalizing relations with Eastern Europe was initiated as early as 1961, when (administered by Foreign Minister Gerhard Schröder and coordinated in every phase with the United States) Chancellor Adenauer's government began to demonstrate more flexibility in dealings with the communist nations on the Continent. The goal of this policy was to expand West Germany's diplomatic relations to the countries of the Warsaw Pact beyond formal ties exclusively to the Soviet Union, which had been established in 1955. This meant that the Federal Republic was prepared to gradually rescind its claim to be the only legitimate successor to the German Reich (a principle which became known as the "Hallstein Doctrine") and eventually to drop it altogether. But Schröder's Ostpolitik was also aimed at keeping the German Democratic Republic isolated, which was the real object of the "Hallstein Doctrine". And this, in turn, prompted the Soviet Union to impede Bonn's efforts to normalize relations with the communist states of Eastern Europe. But West Germany nevertheless was able to exchange trade missions with four of the East Bloc states within a short period of time.

The really significant change, however, came under the Willy Brandt Administration, a coalition government made up of Social and Free Democrats. The emphasis of this "new Ostpolitik" was based on achieving conciliation with the Soviet Union and contained a decisive new element: it was also geared toward bringing about rapprochement with the German Democratic Republic. The intellectual architect and executor of this new political course was Brandt's close advisor Egon Bahr. For several years after the war, Bahr had been Bonn commentator for RIAS (Radio in the American Sector of Berlin), a radio station under official American management. He had also been an advisor and press aide to Willy Brandt during his years as Lord Mayor in Berlin. Bahr was appointed Minister without portfolio in the Brandt government.

The "new Ostpolitik" brought normalization of relations treaties with the Soviet Union, Poland and Czechoslovakia and a „Treaty on Basic Relations between the Federal Republic of Germany and the German Democratic Republic." These steps were accompanied by letters from the Federal Republic stating its unchanged goal to be the unification of Germany and emphazising the special nature of its relationship with the German Democratic Republic which must be governed within the framework of existing FRG treaties and agreements with the three Western Powers and with the Four Powers as far as they remain responsible for Germany as a whole. But the real pillar of this edifice of detente was the Four Power Agreement on Berlin of September 3, 1971. Once again it was American diplomacy that had played a major role in bringing about this agreement.

Aside from its function as the stepping stone to further progress, the Four Power Agreement's significance lies in the fact that the United States, Britain, France and the Soviet Union found a way to improve their special positions in the divided city without changing the status of Berlin, while at the same time securing for the first time on a contractual basis access of German traffic (persons and goods) to and from the Federal Republic and West Berlin. This precludes (at least legally) a repetition of the blockade situation of 1948/49. It is to President Nixon's credit that in the critical rounds of negotiations with the Soviet Union he insisted that the treaty include guarantees for German access to and from the isolated city. These guarantees are contained in the East-West German accords which are tied to the Four Power Agreement.

For the United States and its allies it is important that as a result of this agreement, Berlin is no longer a potential powder keg in every dispute with the Soviet Union. In addition to providing the West Berliners and West Germans with a guarantee of free access, the agreement stipulates that the ties between West Berlin and the Federal Republic of Germany can be maintained and developed. The Four Power Agreement, for which the United States pushed especially hard, has therefore become the most tangible demonstration to date of how detente can be achieved and applied to benefit the everyday person.

The treaties which West Germany has concluded with the nations of the Warsaw Pact since 1970 contain two essential points: factual recognition of existing borders (most significantly recognition of the Oder-Neisse Line as Poland's western territorial boundry); the assurance of all sides that these borders are inviolable and may be changed only through peaceful means; and mutual renunciation of force. In these treaties, West Germany made significant contributions toward relaxing tensions in Europe, even though some of what Bonn decided to accept had long before become a part of the status quo. West Germany's contributions included formal recognition of Germany's territorial losses in Eastern Europe and recognition of the existence of two states in Germany. Bonn has recognized the German Democratic Republic but with some significant reservations: The Federal Republic has not established diplomatic relations with the GDR in the conventional sense of two countries *foreign* to each other. Bonn has relations of a "special nature" with East Germany. In addition, West Germany maintains that the German *Nation* still exists, though it is now divided into two separate states.

As part of the changed political situation and climate which resulted from Bonn's new "Ostpolitik", the Federal Republic of Germany and the German Democratic Republic became full members of the United Nations in 1974. East Germany, which up to then had been almost isolated from the West, began gaining more and more international recognition. The most important step in this development was the establishment of diplomatic relations with the United States, Britain and France, which is tantamount to these countries giving official sanction to the division of Germany. West Germany, for its part, still reserves the right and option of the German people to become reunified through peaceful means. Although this policy is supported by Germany's Western Allies, realization of this hope seems to be far away as long as there are no basic changes in the general situation in Europe.

Aside from some minor differences of opinion between Bonn and Washington on a few details of these agreements and some initial hesitation, the United States eventually gave its sanction to West Germany's Eastern Policy decisions. After all, the Ostpolitik was also in America's interest in that it brought about a reduction of tensions and therewith lowered the probability of crises in Central Europe. There was really only one aspect of Willy Brandt's Ostpolitik that caused some concern in Washington. The experts on Germany in the White House and State Department feared that this policy could cause irreparable antagonism between its Social-Liberal supporters and its Christian Democratic conservative opponents. These experts believed that this could endanger the internal stability of the Federal Republic, something on which America has based its policy on Germany since the end of the war.

As it turned out, these worries were not completely justified, but they continue to exist. The differences of opinion between West Germany's major democratic parties concerning the contents and ways and means of Bonn's Ostpolitik as well as the possibilities for really achieving good-neighborly coexistence are still considerable. The fact that the Warsaw Pact states continue to increase their offensive military strength worries and raises some doubts among both government and opposition politicians. Should the conservative opposition (which has worked toward modifying Brandt's Eastern Policy) manage to return to power again in West Germany, the United States would soon be faced with deciding whether to support or oppose a modification of this policy.

Besides all of the ups and downs and slight variations in German-American history between 1945 and 1975, relations during this period also produced some constants with weight of their own. This is especially true of their economic and military ties. On the basis of a friendship and trade agreement concluded in 1954, and in the course of worldwide economic developments, trade between the two countries reached hitherto unknown proportions.

In 1974, for example, German exports to the United States amounted to 6.7 billion dollars; American exports to West Germany totaled 5.4 billion. The only countries with which West Germany does more business are the five other original members of the Common Market: France, Holland, Italy, Belgium and Luxembourg. Motor vehicles account for an unseemingly high and economically-sensitive portion of West German exports to the United States: forty per cent. Twenty-five per cent of America's exports to West Germany are agricultural goods, such as oil seeds, grain and tobacco. German receipts from services transactions with the United States amounted to five billion dollars in 1973. German payments for services transactions with the United States in he same year exceeded 2.7 billion dollars. It should be noted that the Federal Republic has fully repaid its share of Marshall plan aid.

Since the creation of the European Common Market, American investment in Europe has climbed much more rapidly than European investment in the United States. In 1974, direct German investment in the United States amounted to 3.4 billion German marks (1.4 billion dollars) while American investment in West Germany was five times that amount: seventeen billion marks (seven billion dollars). America's bilateral balance of trade and payments with West Germany has often been passive over the past ten years. But it should be considered that America's exchange of goods with the entire European Community (in which West Germany is the economically strongest member) brought the United States a surplus balance of trade amounting to twenty billion dollars in the short period between the foundation of the EEC and 1974 alone: Bonn is agreed with Washington that the continuing GATT negotiations (General Agreements on Tariffs and Trade) should bring about an even greater liberalization of trade through reduction of non-tariff barriers which still exist on both sides.

The United States and the Federal Republic of Germany are the world's two largest trading nations. In 1974, total American exports were 100 billion dollars and West Germany exported goods amounting to slightly more than ninety billon dollars. But measured in terms of GNP, American exports in 1974 accounted for only 7.5 per cent of the U.S.A.'s gross national product. West Germany's exports in that year, however, accounted for more than 22 per cent of the West German gross national product. This means that the Federal Republic is more dependent on its export trade than the United States, whose gross national product is almost four times as high as that of West Germany.

American investment in the Federal Republic (seventeen billion marks) accounts for almost forty per cent of total foreign investment (1974 = 38.2 billion marks). And there is hardly a branch of business in West Germany in which American firms are not involved. Almost all large American banks have branches in major West German cities. American oil companies dominate the gas station landscape. And in the German grocery, automobile, metal, chemical, electrical and even mail order branches, American businessmen are just as enterprising as a home.

In comparison, the German's share of business in the United States is very modest, though increasing steadily. German businessmen are present on the American market mostly in the fields of synthetic materials, metals and chemicals. It is considerably more difficult for a German than for an American to adapt to business practices and dealing with organized labor in foreign countries. Americans have the advantage of their enormous financial strength, which often gets them additional advantages on foreign markets. And there is no question that the huge American investment in West Germany greatly benefits the U.S. economy.

The United States and the Federal Republic of Germany are probably more intensively intertwined militarily than any two allies have ever been in peacetime. The fact that the new German Army scrapped the old steel helmet which was a symbol of military tradition throughout two world wars and now wears rounder headgear modeled after the American helmet speaks for itself. East German soldiers wear of course a Soviet shaped steel helmet. The organization command procedures of the American and West German Armed Forces are very similar, though the Germans have tapped their own experiences in working out the formation of their army units. The new German Army was initially equipped with tanks, heavy artillery and airplanes by America, which delivered materials valued at about four billion marks (at that time one billion dollars) at no cost to the German government. Up to 1961, West Germany spent about 5.5 billion marks on additional equipment purchased in the United States or built in Germany under American license. In two-year agreements concluded between 1961 and 1975, West Germany appropriated a total of 40.2 billion marks (11.5 billion dollars) for offsetting the currency drain on the U.S. Treasury by the presence of American troops in Germany. Of this, 26.24 billion marks were spent on American military goods.

These offset-agreements were a substantial German contribution to the NATO defense effort in Europe and toward helping America's balance of payments. They were necessary because the American forces stationed in West Germany have expenditures for services which have to be paid by the U.S. Government in German currency. In order to be able to do this, the U.S. Treasury has to buy about two billion dollar's worth of Deutsch marks every years. As a result of the offset agreements, the Federal Republic has offset about eighty per cent of the currency drain, primarily through weapons purchases but also by paying off debts before they were due or by purchasing U.S.

Treasury bonds. The Federal Republic of Germany is the only European member of NATO which has made such offset payments.

The armaments used by the West German Armed Forces are now either being produced in Germany or in joint production with West Germany's European Community partners. The Luftwaffe (air force), for example, will be equipped in the future with the German-Italian-British "multirole combat aircraft" (MRCA). So, as of 1975 the requirements for additional offset-agreements were no longer in effect. Nevertheless, Germany will continue to buy some American-made military hardware. Besides, the American forces are not stationed in the Federal Republic solely for the protection of West Germany but also for the security interest of the United States and the West European NATO members.

In addition to heavy artillery for the army, German military purchases in the Unites States have consisted mainly of airplanes and missiles. In the 1970's, the Luftwaffe was equipped almost exclusively with American weapons systems: the Sergeant, Honest John, Hawk, Nike and Pershing missile systems; fighters, fighter-bombers and reconnaissance planes of various types including F-104 G Starfighters, RF 4 e Phantoms and F 4f Phantoms; transport aircraft such as Boeing 707's, Convairs and Jet Stars, and various trainers and transport helicopters. The navy has a number of American-built destroyers.

All German rocket personnel and almost all of the Luftwaffe's pilots are trained in the United States. Since 1958, a total of 138,500 German soldiers, non-commissioned and commissioned officers have been trained at air bases stretching from the East Coast to Southern California; 114,550 from the Luftwaffe, 20,700 from the Army and 3,300 from the Marine (navy).

The most vital aspect of German-American military cooperation is the continuous stationing of U.S. Forces in the Federal Republic and what amounts to a token force in the American Sector of West Berlin, composed of the "Berlin Brigade" equipped with but a handful of tanks. The bulk of American Forces in Central Europe is made up by the Seventh U.S. Army and Air Force units stationed in the Federal Republic of Germany. Following Germany's unconditional surrender in 1945, approximately two million GI's were on German soil. They were quickly demobilized and the number of troops shrunk to the point at which there were only 83,000 left in Germany in 1949. But the number was increased again as a result of the cold war, the creation of the North Atlantic Treaty Organization and the American Congress' resolution on the stationing of U.S. Forces in Europe. This resolution was prompted by President Truman, introduced in Congress by Republican Senator Arthur H. Vandenberg of Michigan and passed in 1948.

German and American tank officers inspecting a unit in Germany

131

American troop strength reached its first peak in 1954, when exactly 250,000 men were stationed in Germany. It declined again somewhat in the following years but jumped to a new high of 277,000 in 1962 after Khruschev's "Berlin Ultimatum". But as the situation in Europe quieted down and the war in Vietnam took on greater proportions, the number declined steadily. Since 1970, on the average there have been 200,000 American soldiers stationed in West Germany; 23,000 in the Air Force and between 170,000 and 180,000 soldiers in the Seventh Army. In 1974, they numbered exactly 22,000 in the Air Force and 169,000 in the Army.

The soldiers are often accompanied in Germany by their dependents, mostly wives and children. Between 1970 and 1974, the average number of dependents in the Federal Republic was 129,000 wives, children and other relatives.

It is estimated that the rotation of the troops and their dependents between 1948 and 1975 brought two million American soldiers and dependents to West Germany for a period of at least one year, usually for longer. But their contacts to the native population differ greatly. The majority confine themselves to their habitual environment in barracks and "little Americas" on the bases with their own American schools, churches, clubs, supermarkets, theaters and libraries. Public opinion polls show that the Americans are much more liked by the German population than the forces stationed in the Federal Republic by the French, British and Belgians. But usually the American soldier's contact with the Germans is minimal. All conceivable efforts undertaken by both German and American organizations and authorities have failed to do much to change this. The average American abroad seems to prefer staying as close to his native surroundings as possible.

American Forces in Europe are an integral part of NATO with its headquarters in Brussels.

Operational control of the American Forces in the Federal Republic and in Berlin is exercised by the United States European Command (US EUCOM) with headquarters in Stuttgart-Vaihingen. The U.S. Army, Europe and the Seventh Army (USAEUR) is headquartered in Heidelberg, one of the most romantic and loveliest German university cities, surrounded by forests and hills. These ground forces are organized into the V and VII Corps, composed of $4\frac{1}{3}$ divisions, which in 1975 were reinforced by two brigades. One of these two additional brigades has been assigned to Lower Saxony, which belongs to the Allied Forces Northern Sector in Germany. All other American ground and air units are based in the Allied Forces Central Sector in the Federal Republic. The major divisional elements of the Seventh Army are stationed around Goeppingen (1st infantry division), Würzburg (3rd infantry division), Bad Kreuznach (8th infantry division), Frankfurt (3rd armored division) and Ansbach (1st armored Division). Moreover, the 2nd and 11th amored cavalry regiments with a total strength above 6,000 men provide border surveillance. The U.S. Air Forces in Europe (USAFE) headquarters is at Ramstein Air Force Base. Its elements stationed in Germany are under the command of the 17th Air Force, headquartered at Sembach Air Force Base. They are part of the Allied Tactial Air Forces in the Federal Republic with a total of approximately 500 modern first line combat aircraft, mostly F-4, F-111 and A-7.

The NATO Forces stationed in Central Europe have far fewer soldiers and less airplanes and tanks than the rival Warsaw Pact. And even though the quality of NATO's air power and anti-tank defenses is much higher than that of the communist forces, the United States has more than 7,000 tactical atomic weapons in Central Europe (probably 5,000 of them in the Federal Republic) in order to counterbalance the numerical superiority of the Warsaw Pact. The atomic weapons are intended for use by the American and other Allied Forces, including the German Forces, in case of nuclear war or an attack by Warsaw Pact conventional forces of overwhelming strenght. But they are in American custody and can only be used on explicit orders from the American President.

It has not been made public how many of these tactical nuclear weapons are earmarked for use by the German Forces, but it can be assumed that two-thirds of the 7,000 tactical nuclear warheads in Europe would be assigned to non-American Allied NATO Forces. They are for use by the artillery, on short and medium-range anti-aircraft missiles and by fighter-bombers. They have a yield of between 0.1 and 400 kilotons (one kiloton or kt being the equivalent of 1,000 tons of TNT, measured in energy). An observant American tourist could conceivably chance upon a passing motorized German unit and notice that in its center there is a small special unit of Americans; those just might be the GI's carrying tactical nuclear weapons to be turned over to their German partners in the event of war.

There are many official and sometimes even flowery definitions of the task of the U.S. Forces stationed in the Federal Republic of Germany. But even the military greenhorn can deduce why they are here:

1) For the reinforcement and the protection of the Central European NATO Front and to slow down any attack by the Warsaw Pact to gain time in which a decision on how the West should react can be made.

2) As military "hostages" in the sense that an attack on the Seventh Army would be tantamount to an attack on the United States and would therefore provoke full response by the Alliance and the USA.

3) For the cohesion of the NATO Forces. The troops of the other Alliance members are too weak and disunited to hold off an attack, even with the strong German contingent of twelve divisions, but their presence is a psychological deterrent, and with the Americans, they conceivably could contain the superior Soviet Forces, at least for a crucial period.

4) To balance the military weight of the Federal Republic of Germany within the Alliance. Without the presence of the American forces, the German armed forces would constitute a factor of superior conventional strength in Western Europe. This could become embarrassing or irritating for some European members of NATO.

The stationing of American Military Forces in West Germany and Soviet Forces in East Germany has created a certain amount of balance which prevents armed conflicts. But the conglomeration of the strongest, best-equipped and most mobile units of the two rival military alliances on such a small area of Central Europe (the two German states together host about 1.5 million soldiers and thousands of tanks and airplanes), is a direct contradiction of all of the talk and solemn declarations concerning a "relaxation of tensions". It is precisely for this reason that since 1973, the NATO and Warsaw Pact members have been negotiating a mutual reduction of forces. The West would like to agree with the East on a "common ceiling" of military power in Central Europe, so that there would be a balance of forces in East and West and no threatening conventional superiority of Warsaw Pact forces.

The large amount of "military tourism" going on between the United States and West Germany is commensurate with the increasing numbers of civilian tourists crossing the Atlantic. The number of German visitors to America has risen from 36,000 in 1960 to almost 300,000 in 1974. This puts Germany in fourth place on the list of America's foreign vacation guests, right after Canada, Japan and the United Kingdom. Fifty per cent of German tourism beyond the confines of the European Continent goes to the United States. And in the age of charter flights and intercontinental travel, the stream of visitors from West Germany to the United States could be much larger if the American tourist industry would only adjust itself a little more to accomodate the interests and wishes of the foreign visitors. Most of the Germans who fly to the United States belong to the higher income and education groups and most of them return home with friendly feelings.

In the opposite direction, West Germany is a favorite vacation-target of American tourists. In 1973, almost half a million Americans visited the Federal Republic. Almost as many Americans come to West Germany as visit England, and many more than go to Italy, Spain or

American and German soldiers relaxing together after exercise

Romantic Heidelberg, the famous university city in Southern Germany, attracts many American tourists—and scholars

France. In fact, almost as many Americans visit West Germany as Frenchmen and Englishmen. These numbers vary, of course, with overall fluctuations in the world economic situation; since the recession in 1973, fewer American tourists visited West Germany than in the previous years.

Cultural and intellectual exchange between the United States and West Germany is intensive though somewhat more difficult to demonstrate in statistics. This exchange is supported by public and official funds on both sides. There is no question that America has a dominating position in West Germany's entertainment landscape. Over 25 per cent of all films shown in the Federal Republic come from the United States. American film and TV-serial stars as well as jazz and pop musicians are as well-known in Germany as they are at home. The two German television channels are packed with western and detective thrillers from American film studios, including "Bonanza", "Columbo", New York's cop Lt. Kojak and "The Streets of San Francisco". The Germans, for their part, regularly send famous orchestras and ballet groups to perform in large American cities and many German concret solists go on tour in the United States every year.

Somewhat less visible but nevertheless effective in promoting transatlantic exchange of information and culture is the work of the two countries government-financed cultural and information agencies. They supply the interested public with official information, press reviews and documentation and are active organizing cultural events and exhibits.

One of the most efficient institutions of this kind were the fifty "America Houses" which were opened in Germany during the worst post-war period and whose well-stocked libraries provided many a downhearted German with a much-needed escape from reality. And divorced from an official propaganda function, they told Germans about America as it really is in symposium discussions, film showings and lecture evenings. Today most of these "America Houses" have been closed down and continue to exist only in Berlin, Cologne, Frankfurt, Hamburg, Hannover, Munich and Stuttgart. Some were bi-nationalized into German-American Societies.

The German Goethe-Institutes in Boston, San Francisco, New York and Atlanta perform a similar function, but are now more oriented toward culture and language. As a demonstration of thanks for assistance the United States gave the Federal Republic through the European Recovery Program (ERP), the West German government in 1972 established a German Marshall Plan Foundation in Washington with initial financing of 150 million Deutsch marks spread over fifteen years. This foundation (under American direction) studies problems

136

confronting advanced industrial societies, problems of international relations that pertain to the interests of Europe and the United States and it supports the field of European studies.

Another example of remarkable cooperation is the Fulbright Commission. This body was created by the U.S. Government in 1952 and named after Arkansas Senator William Fulbright, for many years Chairman of the Senate Foreign Relations Committee. The Fulbright Commission manages fifty worldwide academic exchange programs. In 1962 and 1974, agreements were concluded between Bonn and Washington covering the German-American segment of the program and since 1964, the German Foreign Ministry has been paying eighty per cent oft its cost. Within the framework of the Fulbright Program, since 1952 nearly 6500 Americans received scholarships in the Federal Republic; more than 5500 German students received scholarships in the United States. In addition to this part of its activities, the Fulbright Commission has special programs for specialized universities, education experts, trade union officials, social workers, librarians and museum curators.

Encouraged by the success of the Fulbright Program and as a contribution to the American Bicentennial, the Federal Republic established in 1975 the John McCloy Fund for German-American Exchange under the auspices of the American Council on Germany. The main purpose of the fund will be to facilitate study tours and German-American conferences by young politicians, journalists and representatives of labor and business.

Among the German institutions which promote cultural exchange with the United States are the German Academic Exchange Service, the Humboldt Foundation, the German Research Association and Inter Nationes. Inter Nationes is a government institution with the mandate of presenting an undistorted picture of Germany abroad through films, photographs, books, exhibits and lectures. Several organizations, most of them private (like the Field Service), are very active in America promoting student exchanges. All in all, the German Embassy in Washington spends between sixteen and twenty million Deutsch marks a year (about eight million dollars) for cultural work.

The close political, economic, military and cultural ties between the United States and West Germany require large diplomatic and consular representations. In addition to its Embassy in Washington, D.C., the Federal Republic maintains Consulate Generals in Atlanta, Boston, Chicago, Detroit, Houston (with a branch office in New Orleans), Los Angeles, New York, San Francisco and Seattle. Both countries have tourist offices and chambers of commerce. The United States is represented in West Germany by its Embassy in Bonn, its

Consulate Generals in Bremen, Düsseldorf, Frankfurt, Hamburg, Munich and Stuttgart, and through the U.S. Mission in West Berlin.

The United States is represented in the German Democratic Republic through its Embassy in East Berlin, which was opened shortly after the two countries established full diplomatic relations in 1974. Former Republican U.S. Senator from Kentucky John Sherman Cooper was appointed America's first Ambassador to the German Democratic Republic. Upon taking up his new post, Ambassador Cooper said in an interview that relations between East Germany and the United States need not affect relations between West Germany and America. The recognition of East Germany by the United States, he pointed out, opened up the possibility for a dialogue with a state long cut off from all but the Communist Bloc.

The German-Americans were both the victims of the two wars between the United States and Germany and the beneficiaries of the ensuing reconciliation and Alliance partnership. In 1901, their organizations had joined together under an umbrella organization called the "National German-American Alliance". After 1914, this alliance spent most of its time and energies fighting for maintenance of American neutrality and engaged in bitter controversies with pro-British Americans who were in favor of American entry into the war on the side of the Western Allies. The outcome of the first world war delivered a death-blow to organized Germanity in America.

Attempts at revival were made beginning in 1933 with the establishment of the "German-American People's League"; (which gained notoriety known simply as the "Bund") led by Nationalist Socialist Fritz Kuhn. But despite all the noise it made, it remained completely without influence. As loyal American citizens, the German-Americans could not be aroused to oppose President Roosevelt's support for the Democracies threatened by Hitler. Since 1945, no attempts have been made emanating from West Germany to organize German-Americans as an ethnic group for the purpose of exerting special influence on American politics.

But much is done to preserve German culture and traditions. In Potomac, Maryland (near Washington, D.C.), for example, there is the only public German school still in existence on the North American Continent. It was founded in 1961 and has about 650 pupils enrolled in classes ranging from kindergarten all the way though senior high school. Many of them are American boys and girls. There are approximately a thousand German Societies in the United States, about a hundred of them in New York City alone. There are Goethe Societies in Pennsylvania and Maryland, weekend schools in the Donau-Swabian tradition, German folklore and clog-dancing clubs (Schuhplattler) and

Octoberfests. The Octoberfests in Baltimore, Maryland, in 1974 attracted more than 10,000 visitors. There are some remnants of what had once been a powerful German press in America in the form of mainly local weeklies with an estimated total circulation of 150,000.

In 1974, there were only about 32,000 college and university students in the USA studying the German language, which is in third place after Spanish and French. This is a decline of over twelve per cent in only three years. But in the same year, in West Germany (which has about one-fourth the population of the United States) ninety per cent of the country's 1.7 million senior high school students had English as a compulsory subject. Fifteen thousand students were studying English and American philology at German universities. An American visitor to Germany has no problems finding an English-speaking German. In America, a German almost needs a microscope to find someone who speaks his native language.

What is the essence of relations between the Germans and Americans of today? That could be subject of long essays summarizing all sorts of opinions from all sorts of people with all sorts of social backgrounds, education and degrees of knowledge about the other country. A very simple answer to this question —and an answer which one can only wish is representative of widespread sentiment— came from Pan American Airlines Captain Jack O. Bennett. Between 1945 and 1974 (when he retired from flying), Bennett piloted 23,000 flights between Berlin and Frankfurt. During this time he married a German stewardess, became Honorary Fire Chief of West Berlin and was named an Honorary Citizen of both Spandau and Tempelhof, two city districts of Berlin. He has established his final home in West Berlin, where he now works as a civil engineer for an American firm. Jack Bennett gave the following reason for settling down in Germany: "I don't have any kind of special love affair with Germany or the Germans. But they have always treated me decently and have been nice to me, and that's why I'm staying here."

The American Bicentennial in 1976 gave an opportunity to leaders of both countries to underline the friendship which has developed between their nations. Thus, during a ceremony in the Paulskirche of Frankfurt on May 15th, 1976, Vice President Nelson A. Rockefeller said: "Today, the bonds of friendship between American and Germany are close and strong and becoming more so every day. Allied in the cause of mutual independence, united with other free Nations in the defense of freedom, we share both a responsibility and a magnificent opportunity to advance the cause of liberty and human dignity in the world."

Chancellor Helmut Schmidt replied in a similar vein: "Our two people would not have achieved this extraordinary degree of understanding that is today the pillar and strength of our relationship, if only our cooperation on the political level, which is indeed based on mutual trust, had been the starting point. Apart from our historical and cultural ties, it is above all the human links that have engendered on both sides of the Atlantic that large measure of identity of political and social values that is today the solid foundation of our friendship."

Literature

Ayres, Leonhard P.	The War with Germany — a statistical summary Washington, Government Printing Office, 1919
Berg, Peter	Deutschland und Amerika 1918—1929, 1963 Matthiesen Verlag, Lübeck und Hamburg
Child, Clifton James	Der Kampf des Amerikadeutschtums gegen den Kriegseintritt der Vereinigten Staaten 1914—17, University of Wisconsin Press, Madison 1939
Compton, James V.	Hitler und die USA (The Swastika and The Eagle) 1967 Houghton Mifflin Company, Boston 1968 Gerhard Stalling Verlag Oldenburg
Department of Commerce	Statistics of German Trade 1909—13 Government Printing Office 1918
Dulles, Forster Rhea	The United States since 1865
Epstein, Fritz T.	Library of Congress Germany and USA — Basic patterns of conflict and understandings
Fest, Joachim C.	Hitler Propyläen // Verlag Ullstein 1973
Fisk, Dr. George M.	Die handelspolitischen und sonstigen völkerrechtlichen Beziehungen zwischen Deutschland und den Vereinigten Staaten von Amerika — 1897 Cotta'sche Buchhandlung Stuttgart
Fraenkel, Dr. Ernst	Amerika im Spiegel des Deutschen Politischen Denkens — Westdeutscher Verlag Köln und Opladen 1959
Grewe, Wilhelm	Nürnberg als Rechtsfrage
Küster, Otto	Ernst Klett Verlag Stuttgart 1947
Jungk, Robert	Heller als tausend Sonnen Das Schicksal der Atomforscher Scherz & Goverts Verlag, Stuttgart 1956
Kurrek, Fritz	Deutscher Schiedsspruch entscheidet letzten Grenzstreit zwischen den USA und Großbritannien in Nordamerika — Auswärtiges Amt, 1974

Kraus, Michael	The United States to 1865 The University of Michigan Press Ann Arbor
Lambach, Dr. Frank	Der Draht nach Washington — Druckhaus Rudolf Müller, Köln 1976
Lawrence, Richard D.	US Force Structure in Europe
Record, Jeffrey	The Brookings Institution, Wash. D. C. 1974
Link, Werner	Die amerikanische Stabilisierungspolitik in Deutschland 1921—1932 Droste Verlag Düsseldorf 1970
Moltmann, Günter	Atlantische Blockpolitik im 19. Jahrhundert Droste Verlag Düsseldorf, 1973
Panhorst, Dr. Karl H.	Deutschland und Amerika — Ein Rückblick das Zeitalter der Entdeckungen, Verlag von E Reinhard — München 1928
Pochmann, Henry A.	German Culture in America 1600—1900 The University of Wisconsin Press, Madison
Pross, Helge	Die Deutsche Akademische Emigration nach Vereinigten Staaten — Duncker und Hum Berlin 1955
Record, Jeffrey	US Nuclear Weapons in Europe The Brookings Institution 1974
Roseman, Samuel	The public papers and addresses of Franklin Roosevelt Harper & Brothers, New York, 1950
Scott, James Brown	A Survey of international relations between United Staates and Germany August 1, 19 April 6, 1917 Oxford University Press — New York 1917
Totten, Christine M.	Deutschland — Soll und Haben Amerikas Deutschlandbild Rütten u. Löening Verlag — München 1956
Vagts, Alfred	Deutsch-Amerikanische Rückwanderung Carl Winter — Universitätsverlag Heidelberg
Wheeler-Bennett, Sir John	The semblance of peace
Nicholls, Anthony	Mac Millan, London, 1972
Williams, T. Harry	A History of the United States
Currrent, Richard N. Freidel, Frank	Alfred A. Knopf, New York, 1961/1962
Zink, Harold	The United States in Germany 1944—1955 D. Van Nostrand Company, Princeton, N. J. 1

The author

Joachim H. Schwelien was born in December, 1913, in Gardelegen, a small rural town west of Berlin.

He studied economics and journalism at the university of Berlin. In 1934, he was arrested by the Gestapo for being a member of an outlawed students organization; later, he was sentenced to $3^1/_2$ years in prison for participating in preparations "to overthrow the Constitution of the Reich" by violence.

Schwelien became a journalist in 1946. After serving as an editor for news agencies, he joined the "Frankfurter Allgemeine Zeitung" in 1954 and was its correspondent in Bonn and in Paris; in 1961, he covered the Eichmann trial in Jerusalem for this newspaper.

He then became correspondent of "Stuttgarter Zeitung" for the United States based in Washington. D. C. Simulteanously, he reported for "Die Zeit" and German radio and tv-stations from America. He also wrote some books on American topics.

In 1975, Mr. Schwelien retired from active journalism and has now restricted his writings to selected topics. —

Published and printed by Bonner Universitäts-Buchdruckerei, Bonn 1976
Reproduction by permission only.